The Weapons of Our Warfare

Mare Allison

Sovereign World

Sovereign World Ltd
PO Box 777
Tonbridge
Kent TN11 9XT
England

Scripture quotations are taken from the HOLY BIBLE,
New International Version. Copyright © 1973, 1978, 1984
by International Bible Society. Used by permission.

ISBN 1 85240 167 2

Typeset by CRB Associates, Norwich
Printed in England by Clays Ltd, St Ives plc.

To Aunt Dottie and Uncle Bob Fidler

Acknowledgements

While books usually bear the name of an author, I suppose few are truly individual efforts. This is no exception. It is not possible to name here everyone who prayed and provided encouragement or practical help, but I thank the Lord for each one.

My husband Casey and our children, Esther, Laurel and Natasha, and our granddaughter, Doris, exhibited the patient endurance of saints.

I am grateful to God for those who helped by contributing learning opportunities, prayer, encouragement and constructive suggestions.

Estelle Berger	Dr Agatha Chan
Rev. Simon Gates	Carol Jordan
Rev. John Lau Sai Tsang	Bob Perry
Shannon Smith	Rev. Becky Trask
Dr Jackie Pullinger-To	Danae Turner

Except for the entirely fictitious stories of Joe and his friend Carl, the anecdotes in this book describe actual events. In all but a few places, I have changed names and omitted identifying features.

Contents

Foreword   11

Chapter 1   **Rescued from the Enemy's Camp**   13
            New Lives
                1. Growing in Love for God
                2. Lives of Repentance
            New Purpose
            This Means War
                1. Safe on the Battlefield
                2. Battles and the Bible
                3. Afraid?
                4. If Jesus Won the War, Why Do We
                   Still Need to Fight?
            New Ministry
                Assigned to Enemy Territory
            Looking for Intercessors

Chapter 2   **Preparing for Battle**   36
            Cleansed and Clothed
                1. Walking in the Light
                2. Kathryn's Choice
                3. Clothed in Christ Jesus
            The Armor of Light
                1. The Full Armor of God

2. The Belt of Truth
3. The Breastplate of Righteousness
4. Feet Fitted with the Preparation of the Gospel of Peace
5. The Shield of Faith
6. The Helmet of Salvation
7. The Sword of the Spirit Which is the Word of God
   Temptation No. 1 – Will you use God's power to meet your own needs?
   Temptation No. 2 – Will you use God's power to validate your ministry or prove your identity?
   Temptation No. 3 – Will you try to do the work of God outside the will of God? Will you avoid the cross?

Chapter 3   **Praying in the Spirit**   68
Our Battle Position – Rest
   Entering into God's Rest
A Man Under Authority
Humility
   1. Moses – the Face-Down Leader
   2. Jesus – Humbled Himself and Became Obedient to Death
Submission and Resistance
Whom Shall I Fear?
Recognizing the Enemy
Flesh or Spirit
   1. Arson in Their Midst
   2. June 4, 1989 – Hong Kong
   3. No 'Lone Rangers'
   4. Led by the Spirit
Do Not Grieve the Holy Spirit
Do Not Quench the Holy Spirit
Test Everything
Making Room for the Holy Spirit

Contents

Chapter 4   **God's Weapons**   109
Offense or Defense?
The Nature of Our Weapons
Not For Us – Judgment and Vengeance
The Name of the Lord
  1. As Belonging To
  2. In Appeal To
  3. In the Authority Of, As
     Representative Of
  4. Not a Magic Word
The Sword of the Spirit, the Word
     of God
  Do Not Shrink from God's Word
Proclamation
Praise

Chapter 5   **More Weapons**   138
Forgiveness
Mercy
Love
  1. Love Drives out Fear
  2. Love Subdues Our Enemies
  3. Love Covers Sin
  4. Acts of Intercession
Blessing
Repentance and Confession
  Moses
Faith

Chapter 6   **Still More Weapons**   171
Remembrance
  1. Memory Assistance
  2. Remembrance and Faith
  3. Remembrance and Healing
  4. Remembrance and the Next
     Generation

Binding and Loosing
  1. Plundering the Strong Man's House
  2. Binding Up the Broken-Hearted
Tearing Down and Building Up,
    Uprooting and Planting
  Nehemiah and his Warrior Builders
Thanksgiving
  Coming into God's Presence
Revelation 12:11
  1. The Blood of the Lamb
  2. The Word of Their Testimony
  3. They Loved not Their Lives so
    Much as to Shrink from Death

Chapter 7   **Avoiding the Enemy's Weapons**   204
Deceiver
Accuser
Murderer
Facing the Enemy

Chapter 8   **Gideon and the Weapons of God**   214
'God is With You, Mighty Warrior'
Only Willing Warriors
Torches and Broken Jars

For Further Reading   224

Foreword

The most important thing that I look for in any spiritual book is whether it makes me want to read *'The Book'*. This book written by Mare Allison and born out of personal experience over the years certainly does not replace or enhance the Bible but gives one an appetite to search the Scriptures and then some practical pointers as to how we might live them out.

I would therefore wholeheartedly recommend this book as a handbook for those who as ordinary people, understand the need to be equipped for war. We see from Scripture what the war is about and who the enemy is and how to prepare. It is written in such a way that those of us who do not feel very learned or very spiritual can not only have great hope that we can participate in and be part of the victory, but even long to.

I have known the author for many years both as a friend and as a spiritual partner. She is just like her book suggests – completely unthreatening and one to whom her friends and colleagues feel they can tell anything. She is completely accepting of where one is spiritually but does not then make suggestions (even those which have been particularly helpful to her), but listens to what God says. I have therefore learnt such a lot about Jesus from her because this is how He acts. That is why I believe that one of the reasons why this book will be so helpful is that it is based upon a character that we can relate to – Jesus. As well as spiritual partnership Mare has, over the years, shown through the way that she has shared her house, her family and her time with extrordinary sacrifice and humour that she has practised living out the word. Because of this she has, as the book suggests, been attacked in the areas where she warns that we may expect attack and we **have** seen her come through victoriously.

Those of us who, in this part of Asia, live and work with Mare and her family are proud to share in our part of the war together. We highly recommend this book to those all over the world who know that the battle is the Lord's but that He has privileged us to fight in His name and play our part too.

Jackie Pullinger-To
Hong Kong

Chapter 1

Rescued from the Enemy's Camp

*'For he has rescued us from the dominion of darkness
and brought us into the kingdom of the Son he loves, in
whom we have redemption, the forgiveness of sins.'*
(Colossians 1:13–14)

New Lives

The sunlight hurt his eyes. He blinked, squinted and
turned his head away. Someone was speaking. Instinctively
he ducked, expecting a beating. But he could hear the
voice, gently talking on and on. Suddenly he realized he
could understand it! '... Transportation will be arranged
for you. At the transit center you'll receive food, new
clothes and medical care – everything you need. You don't
have to be afraid now. You're free.'

Free? Had someone actually come to rescue him? He
couldn't remember not being a prisoner. He could only
dimly imagine what freedom might mean. It was too much
to take in. He felt dizzy.

'What's your name?' the voice asked. There was a long
silence while he struggled to form the answer. 'Joe,' he said
at last. It sounded strange. He just stood there. He had
absolutely no idea what to do now.

Like fictitious Joe, we have been rescued! We have been rescued from the kingdom of darkness and set free to live in the kingdom of light. We used to be prisoners, bound under sentence of death because of our sin, held captive by the prince of darkness himself.

We were rescued by Jesus Christ, God the Son, who humbled himself and became a man. In perfect obedience to God the Father he *'himself bore our sins in his body on the tree, so that we might die to sins and live for righteousness'* (1 Peter 2:24). He died on the cross and was raised from death to life – for us.

When we put our trust in Jesus Christ a marvelous transformation takes place. We actually share in Jesus' death and resurrection. We agree with God's righteous death sentence, and we die to self and sin and death. Through his resurrection we are set free to live new lives for Christ – life that never gets old. We are snatched out of Satan's prison and delivered as brand new sons and daughters into God's beautiful kingdom of light, *'a chosen people, a royal priesthood, a holy nation, a people belonging to God, that [we] may declare the praises of him who called [us] out of darkness into his wonderful light'* (1 Peter 2:9).

While Joe was imprisoned his goal was survival. He kept quiet, avoided confrontation with his captors, and tried to be as inconspicuous as possible. He lived only for himself and regarded even other prisoners as enemies. He hoarded food and anything else that might increase his chance of survival. He tricked people and stole whatever he could get his hands on. He did not fight his captors, but was passive and submissive. He even tried to make friends with them, hoping to gain security and easier conditions. Joe's imprisonment deeply affected his perception and character.

Joe needed lots of help after his release. His freedom

was instantaneous, but learning to live as a free man took time and a lot of adjustment. He had food, clothes and medical care. He slept in a comfortable bed, clean, warm and safe. But he often had nightmares about his harsh cell and the sound of his tormentors coming to get him. He would awaken trembling and perspiring. Joe was also afraid of going hungry. He gorged himself at every meal and furtively carried food away. He was withdrawn and suspicious and he avoided others.

As Christians, this is where many of us begin. We have lived for years as prisoners of war in the enemy's camp. When we are rescued by the Lord of Glory who has won the war by his death and resurrection, we are set free. We march out of the camp of sin and death rejoicing. But we hardly realize that we bring with us perceptions, thoughts and personalities which have been warped and bent by our POW experience. *'Once you were alienated from God and were enemies in your minds because of your evil behavior'* (Colossians 1:21). As we become aware of this, we invite the Lord to begin the awesome task of transforming us into his likeness – to give us the mind of Christ, to teach us how to love God and others, to make us into people who desire his will, his plans, his character, and his glory.

We begin to learn a whole new way of life with new motives, new values, new perceptions, and new responses. The very things that helped us survive in the POW camp of this world are tremendous hindrances to life in the kingdom of God. Hoarding and trickery must give way to generous giving, openness and truth. Hostility and distrust must now yield to peace, hope and faith. Where our personalities have been permeated by the POW camp atmosphere of fear and hatred, we must now allow the Lord himself to flood us with his matchless love.

1. Growing in Love for God

'Jesus replied, "Love the Lord your God with all your heart and with all your soul and with all your mind." This is the first and greatest commandment. And the second is like it: "Love your neighbor as yourself."'

(Matthew 22:37–39)

One day while reading this commandment, I realized I did not love God with all my heart, soul and mind. As a matter of fact, I was not too sure I loved him at all. How could I be a Christian serving the Lord when I could not obey this, the first commandment? I confessed, 'Lord, I hardly even know what it means to love you. Forgive me for disobeying your first commandment. Show me how to love you more – make my love for you increase.'

I looked into God's word and discovered that those who love God obey him – they keep his commandments. I began to take God's commandments more seriously, and stopped focusing only on the ones I was obeying while glossing over those I was not.

I had always tried to avoid repentance. When I felt guilty or troubled about my sins and failures, I usually told God I was sorry, promised him I would do better next time, and pushed the guilty feelings away. After all, those feelings are miserable and depressing, and God wants us to have peace, doesn't he?

But God was working. While reading Luke 7:36–50, God showed me how to grow in love for him. This also changed my attitude towards repentance. The passage tells about a sinful woman who approached Jesus while he was at the home of Simon the Pharisee. Simon and Jesus were in the middle of dinner when the woman began making a scene. She wept over Jesus' feet and wiped the tears with her hair. She kissed his feet and poured perfume on them.

Jesus did nothing to discourage her, and he used the occasion to tell Simon a parable.

Two men were indebted to a certain moneylender. One owed fifty day's wages, and the other owed a year and a half's salary. Neither could pay, so the moneylender canceled their debts. Jesus asked Simon, *'Which of them will love him more?' Simon replied, 'I suppose the one who had the bigger debt canceled.'* Right. Jesus went on to talk about how Simon and the sinful woman had behaved towards Jesus. Simon had certainly not made a fuss over Jesus; he had not even made sure Jesus had opportunity to wash before dinner. Jesus said the woman's extravagant behavior was evidence that her many sins had been forgiven, for she loved much. He went on, *'He who has been forgiven little loves little.'*

I sat up straight. He who has been forgiven little loves little. So he who has been forgiven much loves much! Did I want to grow in love for God and others? Then I needed to experience more of his forgiveness. I learned that the more I come to him in repentance, the more I will love him. My attitude towards repentance changed instantly and permanently. The repentance I used to avoid was now attractive, a path of joy and blessing into the fullness of God's love.

I repented of every sin I could think of, taking time to let sorrow come to full bloom. I waited before the Lord for a sense of his forgiveness and cleansing. When I finally ran out of things to confess, I invited the Lord to search me and uncover more. True to his word, my love for God grew. I was beginning to learn to live a life of repentance.

2. Lives of Repentance

'Jesus said, "Repent and believe the good news!"'
(Mark 1:15)

17

'Repent' is the first word in the gospel. The dictionary says 'to repent' means to 'feel sorry or self-reproachful over what one has done,'[1] but this is not really what repentance is about. Christian repentance is described as turning away from sin and turning towards God.

When we repent, we admit God is right. We are sinners who deserve the death penalty. There is no way we can save ourselves. Even our best acts are like filthy rags before our perfect and holy God. We stop denying sin and making excuses. We admit we are helpless to change ourselves, and we cry out to God to save us.

Jesus said, *'Repent and believe the good news!'* (Mark 1:15). The message that Jesus Christ, holy and sinless, came to this world, suffered, was crucified, and died to take the punishment for our sin is very good news to people who realize they cannot save themselves. It is even better news when we learn that the grave could not hold Jesus Christ. Risen from the dead, he has ascended to heaven and is seated in authority at God's right hand. As we trust him, he transforms us from God's enemies into beloved children of our heavenly Father. And when Jesus ascended to heaven, he did not abandon us to struggle on alone. He sent God the Holy Spirit to be with us and in us, as comforter, guide and teacher. He promises never to leave or forsake us. Good news!

Without repentance, this good news just does not matter. 'So what if Jesus died to save me from sin? My life is going OK. I'm not as bad as other people. I feel pretty good about my life.' If we do not repent, how can we believe?

'Repent and believe . . .' 'Repent' is not here all by itself and neither is 'believe'. It says 'repent **and** believe'. For the good news of Jesus Christ to keep being good news in our lives, our faith must grow. Otherwise our Christian experience becomes old and stale, something we remember rather than actively experience. We must learn to live

lives of repentance. We must actively continue to turn towards God and away from sin. This way, we will continue to grow in grace and in the knowledge and love of God.

When we repent and believe the good news, we begin to live by the Spirit. As we let God deal with us, old behavior gives way to holy living filled with good fruit.

> *'The acts of the sinful nature are obvious: sexual immorality, impurity and debauchery; idolatry and witchcraft; hatred, discord, jealousy, fits of rage, selfish ambition, dissensions, factions and envy; drunkenness, orgies, and the like. I warn you, as I did before, that those who live like this will not inherit the kingdom of God.*
>
> *But the fruit of the Spirit is love, joy, peace, patience, kindness, goodness, faithfulness, gentleness and self-control. Against such things there is no law. Those who belong to Christ Jesus have crucified the sinful nature with its passions and desires. Since we live by the Spirit, let us keep in step with the Spirit.'*
>
> (Galatians 5:19–25)

When we are born again we soon discover that our flesh is at war against the Spirit of God. As long as we remain alive on this earth, the battle continues – right inside us. But as we continue to repent and believe, God's Spirit continues to work inside us, healing us, changing us and making us like Jesus. *'And we, who with unveiled faces reflect the Lord's glory, are being transformed into his likeness with ever-increasing glory, which comes from the Lord, who is the Spirit'* (2 Corinthians 3:18).

Heavenly Father, thank you for sending your Son Jesus Christ to die in my place as punishment for my sin. Thank you for forgiving me. I give you thanks for Jesus' resurrection and his victory over the grave.

Help me, Lord, to live a life of repentance and to grow in faith in Christ Jesus. I invite you, Holy Spirit, to shine your light into every area of my life: my behavior, my attitudes, my habits, my speech, my heart, my mind, my emotions, and my spirit. Search me and bring me to repentance over everything that is not pleasing to you. I admit I cannot save myself. I trust you for forgiveness. I believe that the blood of Jesus Christ will cleanse me from all sin. I trust you to make me grow in love for you and others.

Holy Spirit, please fill me and give me your heart, your attitudes, your thoughts, your speech, your habits and your behavior. Lord Jesus, I want to experience your freedom and victory in my life. I give you permission to do whatever is necessary to accomplish this. In Jesus' name, Amen.

New Purpose

'You are not your own, you were bought at a price.'
(1 Corinthians 6:19–20)

One day Joe learned that he would soon be sent for battle training. He was surprised and somewhat alarmed. He had grown quite comfortable. He had begun to enjoy his new freedom and to think he deserved it. He had heard there was a war, but he had not given it much thought. But now that he had recovered from his imprisonment, his new destination was the battlefield.

With Christians it is the same. We have not been set free from bondage and sin so that we can 'do our own thing'. There is a war on. We have been born again into a battle zone. There is no demilitarized zone, no neutral territory.

There are no non-combatants, no conscientious objectors. Jesus said, *'He who is not with me is against me, and he who does not gather with me scatters'* (Matthew 12:30).

We are on one side or the other. Either we are bound in the kingdom of darkness or we are free, living new lives in Christ Jesus. We are either slaves to sin and death or slaves to righteousness. There is no middle ground. We cannot just say, 'Thank you, Jesus, for saving me from sin and death. I'll just get on with my own life now and do my own thing, if you don't mind.' We can try, but it will not work. Our 'own thing' always results in death. *'There is a way that seems right to a man, but in the end it leads to death'* (Proverbs 14:12). God is not trying to spoil our fun. He is not sitting in heaven waiting for us to slip up so that he can punish us. God is good and he loves us. Sin is our enemy. Sin is what alienates us from God and brings us into bondage.

The world says freedom is doing whatever we want. Webster's Dictionary describes free as 'not under the control of some other person or some arbitrary power; able to act or think without compulsion or arbitrary restriction; having liberty; independent'.[2] But when we look carefully at the Scripture, we find that this is not God's definition of freedom. He says, *'You have been set free from sin and have become slaves to righteousness'* (Romans 6:18). We have not been set free to do whatever we want. Our own way leads only back to the bondage of sin. We used to belong to Satan. Now we belong to God.

> *Just as you used to offer the parts of your body in slavery to impurity and to ever increasing wickedness, so now offer them in slavery to righteousness leading to holiness. When you were slaves to sin, you were free from the control of righteousness. What benefit did you reap at that time from the things you are now*

ashamed of? Those things result in death! But now that you have been set free from sin and have become slaves to God, the benefit you reap leads to holiness, and the result is eternal life. For the wages of sin is death, but the gift of God is eternal life in Christ Jesus our Lord.' (Romans 6:19–23)

We need to reject the world's definition of freedom and accept the real one. We are free – free from sin and death, free to live for God. We are set free and our freedom is **in** Christ Jesus. Our lives are not our own. Jesus Christ has bought us with his own life; he has paid for us with his own blood. We belong to him.

If we want to intercede for others and engage in spiritual warfare, we must face the issue of who is in charge of our lives. This is not something we do only once. The issue of Christ's Lordship in our lives will come up time and time again. And each time we must wrestle with it and settle it.

Living for ourselves, 'doing our own thing', or yielding our lives to sin will lead us back into captivity.

Heavenly Father, I understand that to obey you is perfect freedom and running my own life will bring me into bondage to sin. I confess that true freedom is found in Jesus Christ alone. Forgive me for trying to run my own life. Here is my life; I give it completely to you. I confess Jesus Christ as my Lord and I willingly submit to him as my Lord and my God.

Lord Jesus, I choose to obey your word and to do your will. In you is perfect freedom. I invite you, Holy Spirit, to take control of every aspect of my life. I trust you to enable me to live a life of obedience and to fill me with peace and joy. In the name of Jesus Christ, Lord of Lords, Amen.

This Means War

> *'Your enemy the devil prowls around like a roaring lion looking for someone to devour.'* (1 Peter 5:8)

While a prisoner, Joe suffered bondage and deprivation. Since he posed little threat to his captors, he could survive by taking the path of least resistance and cooperating with his jailers. However, once Joe was no longer bound in harmless submission, he became a potential threat. He was now an object of his former captors' attention and unrestrained hostility. How could he survive? Where could he find protection?

When we determine to let Jesus Christ run our lives, commit ourselves to obeying his word, and move forward in aggressive prayer for others, we quickly discover that we have made ourselves offensive to Satan.

The fact is, as soon as we choose life in Christ Jesus, we are no longer Satan's harmless prisoners. We are his enemies and we are in his territory. *'We know that we are children of God, and that the whole world is under the control of the evil one'* (1 John 5:19).

While we were prisoners of the kingdom of darkness, we got along by cooperating. We learned to live in the shadows and even to use darkness to our own advantage. But now we are citizens of the kingdom of Jesus Christ, the kingdom of light, and we are sons and daughters of our heavenly Father. By virtue of our new citizenship and our new nature, we now threaten the very gates of hell. We are now light in the Lord, objects of Satan's malicious attention.

1. Safe on the Battlefield

As children of God and citizens of heaven, we are no longer **of** this world but we are still very much **in** this world. Satan, the prince of this world, is out to eat us up. Have we been rescued from Satan's camp for this? Where is the life of peace we expected? Maybe we should just go back to bondage. It was not pleasant, but it was something we had learned to cope with. How can we survive, let alone triumph? Is there any safe place on the battlefield?

On an earthly battlefield, the only way to insure safety is to get away from the front line and out of action. But on the spiritual battlefield there is no such place. Front lines are everywhere. We cannot simply retreat until we find a peaceful place of compromise – we will just find ourselves back in the enemy's camp. There is a place of complete safety, but it is not a place where there is no battle. The only safe place on the battlefield is **in Christ Jesus**. *'For you died, and your life is now hidden with Christ in God'* (Colossians 3:3).

Once we discover that we are safe in Christ Jesus, we want to find out just where he is. Ephesians 1:20–22 tells us that after God raised Jesus Christ from the dead he *'seated him at his right hand in the heavenly realms, far above all rule and authority, power and dominion, and every title that can be given, not only in the present age but also in the one to come. And God placed all things under his feet and appointed him to be head over everything for the church.'* Jesus Christ is now seated at God the Father's right hand, in the place of all power and authority. He will stay there until all his enemies have become a footstool for his feet, Hebrews 1:13 and 1 Corinthians 15:25.

Chapter two of Ephesians goes on to say, *'And God raised us up with Christ and seated us with him in the heavenly realms in Christ Jesus'* (verse 6). What an amazing position we have in Christ Jesus. We are completely safe. He is presently sitting in the highest place, the place of all power and authority. No one can threaten his position or depose him. And **we** are seated there together with him. Each believer is part of the church, the body of Christ, Ephesians 1:23, 5:29. Because we are part of his body, what is under Jesus' feet is also under our feet. In Christ Jesus we are safe and secure.

2. Battles and the Bible

'All Scripture is God-breathed and is useful for teaching, rebuking, correcting and training in righteousness' (2 Timothy 3:16). Many Old Testament Scriptures are useful for teaching us about the weapons and strategy of spiritual warfare. We battle spiritual enemies with spiritual weapons for '. . . *our struggle is not against flesh and blood, but against the rulers, against the authorities, against the powers of this dark world and against the spiritual forces of evil in the heavenly realms'* (Ephesians 6:12).

Some people are uncomfortable with the whole idea of spiritual warfare. They can accept the God of love as portrayed in the New Testament, but they have trouble relating to the Old Testament God of blood and battles. Some people say the reason there is so much warfare in the Bible is because the people in Old Testament times had only a shadowy and imperfect understanding of who God is. They did not realize that God is love. Other people explain that God's way of dealing with man has changed because we are now living in a different dispensation than people in the Old Testament. Others avoid the difficulty by reading only the New Testament. They view the Old Testament only as a historical record. Still others believe God has changed or that the God of the Old Testament is actually a different God from the God of the New Testament. They feel close to Jesus but far from the God who gave the commandments on Mount Sinai in the voice that thundered.

It may be helpful to consider another view of the Old Testament as it relates to the topic of spiritual warfare. Do these stories of long ago and far away really have anything to do with us? Why pay any attention to these accounts of ancient kings, armies, battles, blood and gore?

Romans 15:4 says that *'everything that was written in the past was written to teach us, so that through endurance and the encouragement of the Scriptures we might have hope.'* Concerning Old Testament events Paul writes, *'Now these things occurred as examples to keep us from setting our hearts on evil things as they did ... These things happened to them as examples and were written down as warnings for us, on whom the fulfillment of the ages has come'* (1 Corinthians 10:6, 11). The things that happened to the people of the Old Testament happened for us, to teach us.

For us? While we may have some real difficulty relating to the lives of ancient people who lived far away, everything changes when we look at them with spiritual eyes. Since our topic is spiritual warfare, let us take a look at some Old Testament battles.

Jericho (Joshua 6), for instance, was not your ordinary battle. Battle strategy involved walking around the city sounding trumpets once a day, for six days. On the seventh day, they walked around it seven times. The seventh time around, they blew trumpets and shouted. Strange battle plan, strange weapons, strange results. The city wall fell down. This was not an ordinary battle – it was a spiritual battle fought with spiritual weapons.

Consider how Gideon and only three hundred men routed an army of 135,000 without drawing their swords (Judges 6–8). And what about David, a shepherd boy not old enough for military service? He felled a giant and put the entire Philistine army to flight with one well-aimed stone (1 Samuel 17). And what about Jehosophat, the king of Judah (2 Chronicles 20)? He assigned singers praising God to the front lines, and the armies of Moab and

Ammon were completely destroyed. These were not ordinary battles. They were spiritual battles fought with spiritual weapons.

3. Afraid?

Spiritual battle need not frighten us. Our defense, protection, authority, victory, armor and weapons are all found in the perfect person and completed work of Jesus Christ. There are three spiritual areas where we find ourselves engaged in warfare: the heavenly realms, the world, and the flesh. Jesus' victory over all these is complete and assured.

Christ's victory is complete over all the powers of Satan. *'And having disarmed the powers and authorities, he made a public spectacle of them, triumphing over them by the cross'* (Colossians 2:15).

Christ has secured victory over the world. The whole world may be under the control of the evil one and it may give us trouble. *'But take heart!'* says Jesus, *'I have overcome the world'* (John 16:33).

Even our own flesh, sin and death have been overcome in Christ Jesus. His victory is sure and complete.

> *'I have been crucified with Christ and I no longer live, but Christ lives in me. The life I live in the body, I live by faith in the Son of God, who loved me and gave himself for me.'* (Galatians 2:20)

> *'For we know that our old self was crucified with him so that the body of sin might be done away with, that we should no longer be slaves to sin – because anyone who has died has been freed from sin.'* (Romans 6:6–7)

The outcome of this war is certain. Christ has already won the victory. Jesus Christ is King of Kings and Lord of Lords. Everything we need is found in him. The more completely we learn to live **in** Christ Jesus, the more we will experience his protection, provision, and victory.

> *'As for God, his way is perfect;*
> *the word of the Lord is flawless.*
> *He is a shield*
> *for all who take refuge in him.*
> *For who is God besides the Lord?*
> *And who is the Rock except our God?*
> *It is God who arms me with strength*
> *and makes my way perfect.*
> *He makes my feet like the feet of a deer;*
> *he enables me to stand on the heights.*
> *He trains my hands for battle;*
> *my arms can bend a bow of bronze.*
> *You give me your shield of victory;*
> *and your right hand sustains me;*
> *you stoop down to make me great.*
> *You broaden the path beneath me,*
> *so that my ankles do not turn.* (Psalm 18:30–36)

God promises us everything we need for battle and gives us the assurance of victory. He is our shield, our Rock, and our strength. He makes us able to do battle. He promises us strength and victory; he will keep us from falling. Shall we trust him and go forward to take enemy territory? Or will we choose to live as if we are still prisoners of war, defeated, bound and afraid, but comfortable with the familiar?

4. If Jesus Won the War, Why Do We Still Need to Fight?

When we begin to seriously consider spiritual warfare, another question arises. Since Jesus Christ has already secured victory by his death and resurrection and since he is seated at the right hand of the Father, ruling and reigning with him, why do we still need to fight? *'In putting everything under him, God left nothing that is not subject to him. Yet at present we do not see everything subject to him. But we see Jesus...'* (Hebrews 2:8–9). At this point we do not yet see everything subject to Jesus Christ. We are called to continue obedient in faith until the rule and reign of Jesus Christ are fully manifested in all creation, until all his enemies are under his feet.

When a king ascends to his throne, he is anointed, proclaimed as king, and his rule is established. His ascension is announced with trumpets. Messengers are sent into every corner of the kingdom, proclaiming the rule and reign of the king. Jesus Christ is the King. He has died, been buried and has risen again. He has ascended to the Father. He is seated enthroned at God's right hand. He is waiting until the good news of his ascension and of his rule and reign of righteousness and mercy have been announced in all the ends of the earth.

We are to blow the trumpet, shout aloud, and announce the Good News of the King Jesus Christ into every dark corner of the kingdoms of this world. We must not hesitate or hold back.

When the announcement of the king is made, suppose there are some rebels who refuse to recognize and obey the king. What does the king do? He sends his soldiers to claim back the rebel territory and to release the prisoners. This continues until his entire kingdom is fully subject to him.

This is exactly what Christians are to do today. We announce the good news of Jesus Christ to those in captivity, and we go forward into spiritual battle, opposing Satan's powers in the heavenly realms. He is holding territory and souls which rightfully belong to Jesus Christ. We are to take them back. We do this by prayer and intercession on behalf of others and by spiritual warfare in the heavenly realms as well as by proclamation of the gospel to those on earth.

> Father in heaven, I thank you for your mighty power which you exercised when you raised your son Jesus Christ from the dead and seated him at your right hand, far above all rule, authority, dominion and power (Ephesians 1:20–21). Thank you for making me alive in Christ and for seating me together with him. I thank you that in Jesus I am safe and secure. I depend upon you alone to protect me. I proclaim the victory of Jesus Christ over sin and death, the world and all the powers of Satan.
>
> Lord, I ask you to teach me to stand firm against all the devil's schemes. Teach me to advance, claim territory for you, and see you set captives free. Teach me to be alert and to always keep on praying. May your kingdom come and your will be done on earth as it is in heaven. I ask these things in the name of the Lord Jesus Christ who is seated at your right hand and is ruling and reigning forever. Amen.

New Ministry

'We are therefore Christ's ambassadors.'
(2 Corinthians 5:20)

Along with new lives and a new purpose, we have a new assignment. Christians are Christ's ambassadors. An ambassador represents his own government in a foreign country. His character and behavior are important because he stands as his nation's representative. Not only must he accurately communicate the wishes and policies of his country's leadership, but also he personally represents the country and its leader. He must share his leader's purpose and vision and reflect his standard of behavior.

When we consider that it is God himself whom we represent, we may wonder if God knows what he is doing. 'Surely there must be some mistake, Lord. Me? I'm just an ordinary Christian. I do the best I can, but I'm not ambassador material.' But 2 Corinthians 5:14-21 describes how the Lord equips us to be Christ's ambassadors. He has given us new hearts which he fills with his love. Our innermost motivation is changed. We serve him as his ambassadors because '... *the love of Christ compels us*' (2 Corinthians 5:14).

Having hearts compelled by Christ's love affects our behavior. An earthly ambassador must always consider how his words and actions will reflect upon his country and leader. He must be a diplomat twenty-four hours a day. So it is with us, but as Christ's ambassadors we have an advantage. Our whole lives already belong to him. He fills us with his love and expresses himself through us by his Spirit. No longer do we live to fulfill our own selfish purposes. We live for him. '*And he died for all, that those who live should no longer live for themselves but for him who died for them and was raised again*' (2 Corinthians 5:15).

As Christ's ambassadors, God gives us spiritual eyes through which we can see others, including Jesus himself. '*So from now on we regard no one from a worldly point of view. Though we once regarded Christ in this way, we do so no longer. Therefore, if anyone is in Christ, he is a new creation; the old has gone, the new has come!*' (2 Corinthians 5:16, 17). We can see each other with the eyes of Christ. How wonderfully God has equipped us in Christ to represent heaven's point of view.

Ambassadors speak as instructed, never airing their personal opinions. They have authority to speak on behalf of the one who has sent them and they communicate his message. Likewise, God has given us his authority and his message: *'And he has committed to us the message of reconciliation. We are therefore Christ's ambassadors, as though God were making his appeal through us. We implore you on Christ's behalf: Be reconciled to God'* (2 Corinthians 5:19–20).

Assigned to Enemy Territory

Earthly ambassadors serve only in friendly countries. At the onset of any hostilities, the ambassador is immediately withdrawn. Not so heaven's ambassadors. Christ's ambassadors are intentionally assigned to enemy territory. The spiritual government of this world and its leader, Satan, are violently opposed to the government of our Lord and God, Jesus Christ.

As Christ's ambassadors, we can assist those in enemy territory in two ways. Firstly, we implore with them to be reconciled to God, to escape from the kingdom of Satan through Jesus Christ. Secondly, we pray and plead on their behalf before God's throne of grace. Prayer is an activity which reaches into the spiritual realms. As we exercise this ministry of reconciliation we soon find ourselves in the midst of an intense battle in the spiritual realm. When we pray, we stand in direct opposition to Satan and his purposes. When he finds he cannot destroy us, he will try to scare us into inactivity, incite us to sin, or simply wear us down with discouragement. We need to be as much warriors as ambassadors.

In some measure, earthly ambassadors also act as representatives of the people of the country in which they serve. They are in a position to act as intercessors. The dictionary says to intercede is 'to plead or make a request in behalf of another or others' and 'to intervene for the purpose of producing agreement; mediate'.[3] Intercession is an integral part of the ministry of reconciliation. We plead with men on God's behalf to be reconciled to him through Jesus Christ. We plead with God himself on men's behalf for grace and mercy. This pleases God because he is looking for intercessors.

Looking for Intercessors

> *'I looked for a man among them who would build up the wall and stand before me in the gap on behalf of the land so I would not have to destroy it, but I found none.'*
> (Ezekiel 22:30)

God the Father is looking for intercessors. In Isaiah 59 we read about a nation in difficulty. People had become so blind that they could not recognize justice even if they fell over it. *'So justice is driven back, and righteousness stands at a distance; truth has stumbled in the streets, honesty cannot enter. Truth is nowhere to be found, and whoever shuns evil becomes a prey'* (Isaiah 59:14, 15).

The problem was sin. *'But your iniquities have separated you from your God; your sins have hidden his face from you so that he will not hear'* (Isaiah 59:2). People were lying, doing evil, and rebelling against the Lord. There was no justice and no one cared except God.

> *'The Lord looked and was displeased that there was no justice. He saw that there was no one, he was appalled that there was no one to intervene; so his own arm worked salvation for him, and his own righteousness sustained him.'*
> (Isaiah 59:15, 16)

God was looking for someone to intervene, someone to intercede, someone to stand in the gap and bring reconciliation. He found none. When nobody could do anything, God worked salvation with his own arm.

A little study with the help of a concordance tells us more about God's right arm. For example, look at Isaiah 53, the well-known passage about the sufferings of Christ: *'Who has believed our message and to whom has the arm of the Lord been revealed? ... He had no beauty or majesty ... He was despised and rejected by men ... But he was pierced for our transgressions ... the Lord has laid on him the iniquity of us all.'* Jesus Christ is the arm of the Lord. Psalm 98:1 says God's right hand worked salvation for him. Psalm 110:1, Luke 22:69, and Ephesians 1:20 place Jesus Christ at God the Father's right hand. How did God find someone to intervene, to intercede? He sent his own Son, Jesus Christ.

Jesus Christ is now seated at God's right hand. What is he doing there? Romans 8:34 says, *'Christ Jesus, who died – more than that, who was raised to life – is at the right hand of God and is also interceding for us.'* Jesus Christ's present ministry is intercession. Hebrews 7:25 says that Jesus *'always lives to intercede'* for us. Since we are seated together with him (Ephesians 2:6), then it follows that our present ministry in God's presence also involves intercession.

Not only are the Father and Son interested and involved in intercession, but so is the Holy Spirit. We are not left to struggle alone in the task of intercession. The Holy Spirit joins with us, helps us, leads us, and even intercedes for us.

'In the same way, the Spirit helps us in our weakness. We do not know what we ought to pray, but the Spirit himself intercedes for us with groans that words cannot express. And he who searches our hearts knows the ind of the Spirit, because the Spirit intercedes for the nts in accordance with God's will.'

(Romans 8:26–27)

God the Father, God the Son and God the Holy Spirit
are all actively involved in intercession. God the Father
seeks intercessors. Jesus' present ministry is intercession.
The Holy Spirit is the Spirit of intercession. As those who
belong to him, is there any question that we also are to
intercede?

> Heavenly Father, I commit myself to be your
> ambassador. Teach me to represent you in my
> actions, words, manner of life and character. Teach
> me to faithfully proclaim your good news. Show me
> how to rescue those bound in darkness. I hear your
> call for intercessors and I put myself at your service.
> Amen.

Notes

1. *Webster's New World Dictionary of the American Language,*
   Second College Edition. World Publishing Co., 1980, p. 555.
2. *Ibid.* p. 1205.
3. *Ibid.* p. 733.

Chapter 2

Preparing for Battle

*'You are all sons of the light and sons of the day. We
do not belong to the night or to the darkness.'*

(1 Thessalonians 5:5)

Cleansed and Clothed

After Joe was freed from the enemy's camp and set free, he
received medical treatment and was given time for rest and
healing. Next he was sent for battle training. He learned
about warfare and what to expect in battle. He was given a
uniform and taught how to manage daily life in battle
conditions. He received armor and training in the function
and care of each piece.

Christians engaging in spiritual warfare also receive
new clothes and armor. We need to learn about the
nature of the battle that faces us and how to function in
battle conditions.

Just what kind of battle are we facing? How do we
perceive it and how do we fight? Ephesians 6:12 says,
*'... our struggle is not against flesh and blood, but against
the rulers, against the authorities, against the powers of this
dark world and against the spiritual forces of evil in the
heavenly realms.'* Our enemies are not flesh and blood

36

enemies. The enemies we oppose and fight against are never other people.

Our enemies are the evil spiritual powers who operate in this world and in the spiritual or heavenly realms. Satan is their lord. He wants to usurp God's throne, the seat of all power and authority. His desire is to draw all worship, attention, and recognition to himself. In order to accomplish this Satan uses the weapons of darkness. He murders, kills, destroys, lies, deceives, slanders, and accuses.

By contrast, we are to be children of the light. We are to walk in the light wearing the armor of light. The source, operation and effects of our weapons are completely different from those of Satan and they are unquestionably superior.

When Joe went for battle training, the emphasis placed on a seemingly mundane lesson entitled 'Battlefield Hygiene' surprised him. He learned that personal cleanliness was very important. Small wounds and scratches which he might ordinarily ignore would need special attention on the battlefield. In the stressful, unhygienic conditions of battle even small wounds can easily become infected and render a strong soldier powerless.

Joe got the message. Even in the filthy environment of the battlefield he must pay close attention to cleanliness, lest he become a battlefield casualty – felled not by enemy fire but by his own personal dirt.

So it is on the spiritual battlefield. Regular attention to personal spiritual hygiene is a must. The spiritual battlefield may be a dirty place, but God's warriors must be committed to confession of sin and to receiving God's continual cleansing. We must choose to walk in the light.

1. Walking in the Light

The Bible declares, *'God is light and in him is no darkness at all'* (1 John 1:5). Jesus plainly stated, *'I am the light of the world'* (John 8:12). He said, *'I have come into the world as a light, so that no one who believes in me should stay in darkness'* (John 12:46). Jesus also said, *'You are the light of the world'* (Matthew 5:14). If we are in Christ Jesus, we are in the light and we are children of light.

Jesus told Nicodemus that mankind naturally hates the light and refuses to come to the light because it exposes his evil deeds (John 3:19–21). Isaiah confesses, *'All of us have become like one who is unclean, and all our righteous acts are like filthy rags'* (Isaiah 64:6). But we can praise the Lord that through Jesus Christ God has called us *'out of darkness into his wonderful light'* (1 Peter 2:9).

We are no longer children of darkness. We are children of the light, children of God. Children of light must live and walk in the light. We must refuse to have anything to do with the works of darkness. No only that, we must actively expose them.

> *'For you were once darkness, but now you are light in the Lord. Live as children of light (for the fruit of the light consists in all goodness, righteousness and truth) and find out what pleases the Lord. Have nothing to do with the fruitless deeds of darkness, but rather expose them. For it is shameful even to mention what the disobedient do in secret. But everything exposed by the light becomes visible, for it is light that makes everything visible. This is why it is said, "Wake up, O sleeper, rise from the dead, and Christ will shine on you."'*
> (Ephesians 5:8–14)[1]

How can we continuously live and walk in the light. How do we expose the deeds of darkness? 1 John 1:5–7 explains:

> *'This is the message we have heard from him and declare to you: God is light; in him there is no darkness*

*at all. If we claim to have fellowship with him yet walk
in the darkness, we lie and do not live by the truth. But
if we walk in the light, as he is in the light, we have
fellowship with one another, and the blood of Jesus, his
Son, purifies us from all sin.'*

When we walk in the light, we allow sin to be exposed.
How uncomfortable – naked, exposed, no secrets, all laid
bare, our heart's innermost secrets out in the open. But
God does not leave us this way. *'If we confess our sins, he is
faithful and just and will forgive us our sins and purify us
from all unrighteousness'* (1 John 1:9).

As soon as my sin is exposed, I have a choice. I can
cover it up again, hiding it from myself and others in an
attempt to regain some sense of comfort and self-respect.
Of course, this will build layer upon layer of secret sin,
willfully hidden away. I may be able to make sure none of
it shows on the surface. I may promise God I will not do it
again and resolve to try harder. But each layer of sin brings
a deeper bondage to sin. I shrink away from the light and
inch from shadows into the gloom and from gloom into
darkness. I try to hide from God, but it is really no use. I
may succeed in deceiving myself and others, but there is
no fooling God.

There is another way. I can choose to acknowledge my
sin and confess it. When I do this, a marvelous thing
happens: The blood of Jesus Christ purifies me. God
forgives my sin and cleanses me completely. How
wonderful! The power of sin is broken. I am free to walk
in the light and sin is gone. I do not need to hide in the
shadows. I can experience continuous cleansing from sin
and uninterrupted fellowship with God and man.

2. Kathryn's Choice

Kathryn filled mugs with steaming coffee and sat down

opposite me. A missionary, she and her husband had been on their assigned field for a number of years. But Kathryn now refused even to speak to her colleagues living in the same building.

I talked to her about walking in the light, repentance and forgiveness. She looked me straight in the eye. 'One day while I was praying and meditating,' she said, 'suddenly I found myself looking at a whole lot of garbage, things about myself that were really painful. It was terrible. Then I realized – I don't have to look at this! I don't have to put up with this. God doesn't want me to be miserable. He doesn't want me burdened down looking at a lot of negative stuff. So I turned my back on it and have never looked at it again.'

Kathryn went on to tell me that she would forgive her fellow missionaries only if they repented, admitted they were wrong and asked her for forgiveness. I explained that the Bible teaches that no matter who is wrong, the responsibility to forgive always lies with each of us. Kathryn disagreed.

In an attempt to illustrate I asked Kathryn how she managed conflicts between her children. 'Suppose they have a disagreement and one is clearly in the wrong but is unwilling to admit it and ask the other for forgiveness. What do you do?'

'I tell him, "Don't forgive him – wait till he admits he's wrong and asks to be forgiven. He doesn't have to forgive."' Stunned by her answer, I was speechless.

Within two years Kathryn and her family left the mission field because of damaged relationships. She was still refusing to speak with her neighbors.

I am convinced that much of Kathryn's difficulty was directly related to her willful choice not to look at sin and come to repentance. Since Jesus had died for her sins, she reasoned, she did not need to look at them. When she turned away from facing her own sin that day, she also turned away from the light. Rather than remaining in the light and dealing with what she saw by repentance and faith in Jesus, she moved into the shadows. She became progressively less sensitive to sin and the need for personal repentance in her own life. She forgave others only when they admitted they were wrong and she taught her children to do the same. Important relationships broke down under the burden of unforgiveness. Kathryn and her family became battlefield casualties, retired by wounds that could have been cleansed and healed – victims of battlefield dirt and poor spiritual hygiene.

Unexpected visitors occasionally come to my home. I love visitors, but sometimes I look at the condition of my house and shudder. 'Dust bunnies' in the corners, 'fall-out' from lunch and unwashed dishes are only too obvious. I feel embarrassed, but there is no time for a quick clean-up. In the evening, sometimes I try to hide the dirt by dimming the lights. While bright daylight reveals dirt all too clearly, in dim lighting even a lot of dirt may escape notice.

Now this tactic works fine for unexpected guests coming to a dirty house, but what about the spiritual dirt in the house which is my life? Will I choose to simply move away from him who is the Light in order to cover my sin? Or will I choose to come to the Light and let him expose the full extent of my sin? Will I let God do this even when others are sure to see? Will I allow God to lay me bare and cleanse me with the purifying blood of Jesus?

In a vision, the prophet Zechariah saw Joshua the High Priest standing before God. Not only was God's blazing light shining on Joshua, showing clearly all his sin, but Satan was also there to accuse.

'The Lord said to Satan, "The Lord rebuke you, Satan! The Lord, who has chosen Jerusalem, rebuke you! Is not this man a burning stick snatched from the fire?"

Now Joshua was dressed in filthy clothes as he stood before the angel. The angel said to those who were standing before him, "Take off his filthy clothes." Then he said to Joshua, "See I have taken away your sin, and I will put rich garments on you."

Then I said, "Put a clean turban on his head." So they put a clean turban on his head and clothed him while the angel of the Lord stood by.'

(Zechariah 3:2–5)

How wonderful! When God shines his light on us and exposes our filth, when Satan is standing there to accuse, God does not leave us naked and condemned. When we come into the light and repent, we receive cleansing with the blood of his own Son, Jesus Christ. He rebukes Satan, washes away our filth, and gives us clean and fine garments.

3. Clothed in Christ Jesus

'You are all sons of God through faith in Christ Jesus, for all of you who were baptized into Christ have clothed yourselves with Christ.'   (Galatians 3:26–27)

A study of the garments God gives us in Christ Jesus is rich fare for meditation. Jesus Christ himself is our righteousness, our garment, our covering and our protection. Here are some references for further study:

Garments of salvation (Psalm 132:16; Isaiah 61:10)
Garments of splendor (Isaiah 52:1)
Robe of righteousness (Isaiah 61:10)
Rich garments (Zechariah 3:4)

Wedding clothes (Matthew 22:11)
Best robe (Luke 15:22)
White clothes/robes (Revelation 3:5, 18, 4:4, 7:9)
Fine linen (righteous acts) (Revelation 18:9)
Clothed with joy (Psalm 30:11)
Garment of praise (Isaiah 61:3)
Lord Jesus Christ (Romans 13:14)

As children of light, we must remain in the light. We must live and walk in the light. Our defense is in Christ Jesus alone. He is the Light! We must live in him.

'Blessed is he
whose transgressions are forgiven,
whose sins are covered.
Blessed is the man
whose sin the Lord does not count against him
and in whose spirit is no deceit.
When I kept silent,
my bones wasted away
through my groaning all day long.
For day and night
your hand was heavy upon me;
my strength was sapped
as in the heat of summer.
Then I acknowledged my sin to you
and did not cover up my iniquity.
I said, "I will confess
my transgressions to the Lord" –
and you forgave
the guilt of my sin.
Therefore let everyone who is godly pray to you
while you may be found;
surely when the mighty waters rise,
they will not reach him.

You are my hiding place;
you will protect me from trouble
and surround me with songs of deliverance.'

(Psalm 32:1–7)

Father in heaven, I acknowledge that my life and protection are in the Lord Jesus Christ. Thank you for covering my nakedness, cleansing me with the blood of Jesus Christ and providing rich, clean garments for me to wear. Thank you that I can stand in your presence – clean, forgiven and clothed.

Lord, I choose to walk in the light. In your mercy may there be no shadows and no dim light. Holy Spirit, I invite you to *'Search me, O God, and know my heart; test me and know my anxious thoughts. See if there is any offensive way in me, and lead me in the way everlasting'* (Psalm 139:23–24).

The Armor of Light

'The night is nearly over; the day is almost here. So let us put aside the deeds of darkness and put on the armor of light.'   (Romans 13:12)

Joe learned the name and use of each piece of armor. He did not put it on only when under attack. He wore it all the time. At first it seemed troublesome, restrictive and clumsy, but soon he felt uncovered and vulnerable without it.

Webster's dictionary defines armor as 'covering worn to protect the body against weapons'.[2] The very fact that God has provided us with armor should be enough to make us realize that we are likely to come under attack. As soldiers on the spiritual battlefield, we must learn to wear and maintain the armor God has given us. We cannot store it away and expect to have time to get it, repair it and put it on when we begin to experience spiritual attack. We must learn to live in it.

The armor God gives us is very special. Did you know that God gives us the armor he himself wears? In Isaiah 59, God is distressed over the sin of his people: wicked lips, feet that rush into sin, evil thoughts, people stumbling in darkness, rebellion and treachery, and the lack of justice and truth. Unable to find an intercessor, God does the job himself. He puts on his breastplate of righteousness and helmet of salvation (verse 17). He intervenes, forgiving those who repent. He acts as an intercessor.

God also wears garments of vengeance and a cloak of zeal as he repays his enemies with judgment and wrath. God reserves vengeance and judgment for himself, but he freely gives us his helmet of salvation and breastplate of righteousness (Romans 12:17–21; 1 Corinthians 4:5).

God's breastplate of righteousness and his helmet of salvation are two of the pieces of armor that we are commanded to put on in Ephesians 6. God puts them on to accomplish his work as intercessor. It should come as no surprise, then, that Ephesians 6 emphasizes prayer. The spiritual warrior is an intercessor. The armor God provides is effective protection for those who battle in prayer for others.

Teaching on spiritual warfare is often limited to a discussion about armor. Application seems distant and attempts to make the teaching practical with 'putting on the armor' prayers can be either magical or mechanical. There are two scriptural keys which can help us translate the armor of God from theoretical to practical terms. We find these keys in Romans 13:12–14:

> *"The night is nearly over; the day is almost here. So let us put aside the deeds of darkness and put on the armor of light. Let us behave decently, as in the*

daytime, not in orgies and drunkenness, not in sexual immorality and debauchery, not in dissension and jealousy. Rather, clothe yourselves with the Lord Jesus Christ, and do not think about how to gratify the desires of the sinful nature.'

The first key is to remember that this is the armor of light. There is no way we can wear the armor of light if we walk in the dark, practice the works of darkness, or cling to the shadows. The armor of light can be worn only by children of light who walk in the light.

The second key is that Jesus Christ himself is our armor. Each piece of armor speaks about an aspect of our relationship with Jesus Christ. When we wear this armor we are living **in Christ Jesus**. When we wear the armor of light, we clothe ourselves in the Lord Jesus Christ.

1. The Full Armor of God

'Finally, be strong in the Lord and in his mighty power. Put on the full armor of God so that you can take your stand against the devil's schemes. For our struggle is not against flesh and blood, but against the rulers, against the authorities, against the powers of this dark world and against the spiritual forces of evil in the heavenly realms. Therefore put on the full armor of God, so that when the day of evil comes, you may be able to stand your ground, and after you have done everything, to stand. Stand firm, then, with the belt of truth buckled around your waist, with the breastplate of righteousness in place, and with your feet fitted with the readiness that comes from the gospel of peace. In addition to all this, take up the shield of faith, with which you can extinguish all the flaming arrows of the evil one.

> *Take the helmet of salvation and the sword of the*
> *Spirit, which is the word of God. And pray in the*
> *Spirit on all occasions with all kinds of prayers and*
> *requests. With this in mind, be alert and always keep*
> *on praying for all the saints.*
>
> *Pray also for me, that whenever I open my mouth,*
> *words may be given me so that I will fearlessly make*
> *known the mystery of the gospel, for which I am an*
> *ambassador in chains. Pray that I may declare it*
> *fearlessly, as I should.'* (Ephesians 6:10–20)

In the context of this passage, there are two things this
armor equips us to do – to stand against the enemy and to
pray for others. Each is repeated four times, emphasizing
our twin roles in prayer, as spiritual warriors and as
intercessors.

We will look at each piece of armor and the defensive
role of the sword of the Spirit, the word of God. We will
discuss its offensive use in Chapter 4.

2. The Belt of Truth

> *'Surely you desire truth in the inner parts;*
> *you teach me wisdom in the inmost place.'*
> (Psalm 51:6)

We are to stand with the belt of truth buckled around
our waist. The belt Paul was referring to was a wide belt
designed to protect one's vulnerable internal organs. The
belt of truth is necessary spiritual protection for our
vulnerable inner man. But we can wear the belt of truth
only when we are walking in truth. What about the words
of our mouth? What about convenient half-truths to save
face and 'little white lies'? What about exaggerated
accounts of our success calculated to make us look good
in front of others? What about the false image of ourselves

that we hold up for others to admire? What about the deceptions we practice which, while not technically 'lies', are nonetheless designed to deceive and mislead? What if we allow the Lord to shine his light on our business, work, finances, personal relationships, and innermost thoughts?

There is no such thing as a little white lie or a harmless deception. When we walk in lies, we buckle the belt of deception around our innermost being. Our lies and deceptions will ultimately be exposed in the light of God's eyes. There is no protection in lies – only an increasing bondage to deception. An alarming thing about deception is that it deceives the deceiver (2 Timothy 3:13). *'Do not be deceived: God cannot be mocked. A man reaps what he sows'* (Galatians 6:7). The one who practices deception will end up its prisoner.

How we need the belt of truth, yet not one of us naturally chooses the truth. Jeremiah wept over man's condition, *'Friend deceives friend, and no one speaks the truth ... Their tongue is a deadly arrow; it speaks with deceit. With his mouth each speaks cordially to his neighbor, but in his heart he sets a trap for him'* (Jeremiah 9:5, 8).

Lies and deception are Satan's weapons. Satan himself is a liar and the father of lies (John 8:44). He deceives whole nations (Revelation 20:3). When we lie, we speak Satan's native language (John 8:44). Do we think we can beat him at his own game? Do we really think we can triumph in battle against him using his weapons? However, Satan has no defense against the truth. Lies and deceptions dissolve before God's truth.

We can put on the belt of truth by getting rid of everything that is false – every lie, every hint of deception. We put on the Lord Jesus Christ who is our belt of truth.

John testified of Jesus Christ, *'The Word became flesh and made his dwelling among us. We have seen his glory, the glory of the One and Only, who came from the Father, full of grace and truth'* (John 1:14). Jesus Christ is the truth in person. He told Philip, *'I am the way and the truth and the life'* (John 14:6).

To Pilate Jesus said, *'Everyone on the side of truth listens to me'* (John 18:37). Belonging to Jesus means choosing the truth. Jesus prayed for his disciples, *'Sanctify them by the truth; your word is truth'* (John 17:17). When we choose to accept Jesus Christ as our Lord and Savior, we must also choose to obey his commands. We discard lies and put on Christ. *'Do not lie to each other, since you have taken off your old self with its practices and have put on the new self, which is being renewed in knowledge in the image of its Creator'* (Colossians 3:9–10).

> *'Teach me your way, O Lord, and I will walk in your truth; give me an undivided heart, that I may fear your name'* (Psalm 86:11). Search me, Lord, and expose every area where I have clothed myself with lies or deception. Show me how to cast aside the filthy web of deception and buckle on the belt of truth, for I have chosen your truth; I have chosen Jesus Christ.

3. The Breastplate of Righteousness

'The prayer of a righteous man is powerful and effective.' (James 5:16)

Christians sometimes tell me that they are not able to pray well because they not spiritual enough or because they are not holy enough. Some have simply given up praying. Others persist, but feel defeated, sure that their unworthiness cancels out their prayers and that God does not hear them. Some ask others for prayer saying, 'God won't answer my prayer, but I am sure he'll answer if you pray for me.' This is simply not true.

Obviously, if there is some specific sin that is hindering a Christian's prayers, he needs to confess it and receive forgiveness. *'If I had cherished sin in my heart, the Lord would not have listened; but God has surely listened and heard my voice in prayer. Praise be to God, who has not rejected my prayer or withheld his love from me!'* (Psalm 66:18–20).

But we are talking about a generalized sense of un-righteousness before God. This needs to be taken care of lest we lose heart and give up praying. The protection of our hearts is vital because '... *it is with your heart that you believe and are justified'* (Romans 10:10). The breastplate of righteousness keeps our hearts secure in the belief that Jesus Christ *'was delivered over to death for our sins and was raised to life for our justification'* (Romans 4:25). It is the breastplate of righteousness which will protect us in the assurance that God accepts us and hears our prayers.

We are to stand *'with the breastplate of righteousness in place'* (Ephesians 6:14). Where is it 'in place'? A breastplate protects the chest where the heart is located. This is not an ordinary breastplate, but the breastplate of righteousness. Our hearts are protected by righteousness.

Where does this righteousness come from? Certainly it is not our own righteousness, since *'all our righteous acts are like filthy rags'* (Isaiah 64:6). We do not stand before God in our own righteousness, but in the righteousness of Jesus Christ. We *'are in Christ Jesus, who has become for us wisdom from God – that is, our righteousness, holiness and redemption'* (1 Corinthians 1:30). When we put our trust in Christ, a wonderful transaction takes place. *'God made him who had no sin to be sin for us, so that in him we might become the righteousness of God*' (2 Corinthians 5:21). What an exchange! He takes all our sin upon himself and gives us his own righteousness.

Our prayers are powerful and effective because of Christ's righteousness. We come to God in prayer, protected in the confidence of Jesus Christ's perfect righteousness. What wonderful protection against Satan who constantly accuses.

If we find ourselves accused of unrighteousness when praying, what should we do? We need to check our breastplate of righteousness. Have we been walking in unrighteousness and sin? Then we need to confess and receive forgiveness. Sometimes all we need to do is to remember and proclaim that Jesus Christ is our righteousness.

At times, we can almost imperceptibly shift from trusting in Christ's righteousness to trusting in ourselves. This can happen when we have been walking in obedience to God and he has been answering our prayers. Deep in our hearts an attitude of pride arises and we subtly begin to believe that God will be even more willing to hear our prayers because we are doing so well. 'I am sure God will answer my prayer this time. I must be getting better at praying. After all, Elsie was instantly healed when I prayed for her last week.' Now this may look pretty ridiculous on paper, but deep in the heart it may be quietly entertained until God shines his light on it. Sometimes we discover and let God deal with such thoughts only after we begin to ask why he is not answering our prayers. Then we find that the breastplate of God's righteousness has slipped down or fallen off altogether.

God's mercy is so great that restoration is only a prayer away. We have only to repent of trusting in our own righteousness and he graciously restores to us his breastplate.

Father in heaven, thank you for your perfect provision of righteousness in Jesus Christ. Protect me from the accusations of the enemy. I believe that the righteousness of Jesus Christ is sufficient, allowing me to stand in your presence. I trust you to bring to light any ways in which I am not trusting in Christ as my righteousness or in which I am trusting in my own good works. Lord, I renounce completely trusting in my own righteousness. I choose you, Jesus, as my righteousness. Thank you, Father, for hearing and answering my prayers in Christ Jesus.

4. Feet Fitted with the Preparation of the Gospel of Peace

'How beautiful on the mountains are the feet of those who bring good news, who proclaim peace, who bring good tidings, who proclaim salvation, who say to Zion, "Your God reigns!"' (Isaiah 52:7)

Remember Joe who was rescued from the enemy's camp? He became accustomed to battlefield life quickly, though at first he had trouble sleeping. It was not that he needed the special comforts of home or even a soft bed. He just did not sleep very well with his combat boots on, and keep them on he must. Should his position come under attack, there would be no time to get his boots on. He had to live in constant readiness. His training officer was not the least concerned that Joe might not be getting enough sleep. He even preferred that Joe not sleep too soundly. He wanted Joe to be ready even when he was resting because enemy attacks are often unexpected.

We Christians also need to keep our shoes on, prepared for battle. If we do not, we will be in danger of falling asleep when we should be awake and watching. God wants us to be ready at all times.

Ready? Alert and watching? For what? The readiness which comes from the gospel of peace will prepare us for a number of things. In the context of armor and spiritual warfare, one that immediately comes to mind is to be alert and prepared in case of enemy attack. *'Be self-controlled and alert. Your enemy the devil prowls around like a roaring lion looking for someone to devour'* (1 Peter 5:8).

As soon as we are set free and recognize our position in Christ Jesus, we are no longer helpless prisoners of Satan. We become a threat to him and a target of his attacks. The shoes of the preparation of the gospel of peace will help us stay alert.

Jesus repeatedly emphasized that we must be watching and serving, ready for his return. He wants to find us prepared, obedient, and performing his will.

> *'Be dressed ready for service and keep your lamps burning, like men waiting for their master to return from a wedding banquet, so that when he comes and knocks they can immediately open the door for him. It will be good for those servants whose master finds them watching when he comes. I tell you the truth, he will dress himself to serve, will have them recline at the table and will come and wait on them.'*
>
> (Luke 12:35–37)[3]

No one knows when Jesus will return, but we know he will come at a time when we do not expect him. The readiness that comes from the gospel of peace will keep us alert and prepared for the moment of Christ's return. He will find us with our shoes on, obediently doing his will. His coming will be a wonderful surprise.

Besides helping us to be prepared in case of enemy attack and for Christ's return, this amazing readiness that comes from the gospel of peace will enable us to recognize and act upon every opportunity to share the good news of

Jesus Christ. God's word tells us, *'But in your hearts set apart Christ as Lord. Always be prepared to give an answer to everyone who asks you to give the reason for the hope you have'* (1 Peter 3:15). On call twenty four hours a day, alert to every opportunity, ready with an answer for anyone who asks, 'How do you cope with ... ?' or 'What do you think about ... ?'

Paul gave Timothy the same instruction: *'Preach the Word; be prepared in season and out of season; correct, rebuke and encourage – with great patience and careful instruction'* (2 Timothy 4:2). It seems Timothy was not just to be ready to share his testimony or to whip out his 'Four Spiritual Laws'. He was to be ready to preach any time – in season and out of season. Timothy was also to be ready to come down from the pulpit and get involved in the nitty-gritty of people's problems. Just as Paul wanted Timothy to be ready to give practical help and instruction to individuals who needed his one-on-one encouragement, so God wants us to be prepared. We are to be ready to preach a gospel with shoes on, walking it out in practical individual situations.

God does not expect us to have all the answers. Maybe he does not expect us to have any of them. But as we walk forward, looking to him, a wonderful thing takes place. He pours out his gifts, enabling us to deal with real and sometimes impossible problems. When my friend needs an answer, God may give it through me. When I need help, my friend may be able to speak the word that sets me free. This is the gospel with shoes on. It goes beyond words and includes every kind of practical help and good work.

All this alertness and readiness begins in the place of prayer. Jesus warned his three sleepy disciples, *'Watch and pray so that you will not fall into temptation'* (Matthew 26:41). Jesus taught his disciples always to pray (Luke

18:1). In 1 Thessalonians 5:17 Paul encouraged the believers to *'pray continually'*.

As we choose to be ready in prayer, we will be alert and ready in all the other areas, too. But if we allow ourselves to neglect the discipline of prayer, we lose the cutting edge of readiness in every other area. When we take off our shoes and get comfortable, our whole Christian experience quickly loses its vitality. We no longer look forward enthusiastically for Christ's return. Our zeal to obey and serve God is blunted. We drop our guard against enemy attack. We may fail to see opportunities to share Christ or find that we have no word, no answer. We have been caught on the battlefield with our shoes off, unprepared.

Our readiness in Christ Jesus is forged, strengthened and sharpened in the secret place of prayer. There, hidden from all eyes but God's, we focus attention on him alone. Our desire for him grows stronger and deeper and our communion with him becomes more intimate. We see his face, learn his will, and he gives us his heart. We hear his voice and obedience becomes our delight. God's life flows through us, Spirit to spirit, and he transforms us into his soldiers – prepared, alert and fully armed.

'Let the peace of Christ rule in your hearts since as members of one body you were called to peace' (Colossians 3:15). Our feet are *'fitted with the readiness that comes from the gospel of peace'* (Ephesians 6:15). We have put on Christ Jesus. We stand in him, walk in him and live in his peace, for *'he himself is our peace'* (Ephesians 2:14). Battles are filled with conflict, confusion, overwhelming violence, hatred and fear. But look at our defense! Peace. Look where we can stand: in peace. In the midst of spiritual battle God enables us to stand in the peace of Christ Jesus. He is the Prince of Peace (Isaiah 9:6).

O Lord, Wonderful Counselor, Mighty God, Ever-lasting Father, Prince of Peace, may your government increase and know no end. Make me ready in every way – alert to enemy attacks, awake, serving, and watching for the moment of your return, ready to give an answer and praying continually. May your peace rule my heart and actions. Enable me to stand in your peace in the confusion and violence of battle, in the name of Christ Jesus.

5. The Shield of Faith

'Blessed are you, O Israel!
  Who is like you,
    a people saved by the Lord?
He is your shield and helper
    and your glorious sword.
Your enemies will cower before you
    and you will trample down their high places.'

(Deuteronomy 33:29)

'In addition to all this, take up the shield of faith, with which you can extinguish all the flaming arrows of the evil one' (Ephesians 6:16). Our faith is not some kind of free-floating, unattached faith. It is not faith in faith. It is faith **in** Christ Jesus.

'But because of his great love for us, God, who is rich in mercy, made us alive with Christ even when we were dead in transgressions – it is by grace you have been saved. And God raised us up with Christ and seated us with him in the heavenly realms in Christ Jesus, in order that in the coming ages he might show the incomparable riches of his grace, expressed in his kindness to us in Christ Jesus. For it is by grace you have been saved, through faith – and this is not from

yourselves, it is the gift of God – not by works, so that no one can boast. For we are God's workmanship, created in Christ Jesus to do good works, which God prepared in advance for us to do.'

(Ephesians 2:4–10)

The whole context of faith in this passage emphasizes that Jesus Christ is the object of our faith. We have been made alive **with** Christ, raised up **with** Christ and seated in the heavenly realms **in** Christ. God gave his only Son – Christ is the gift. The gift of God to us is faith in Christ Jesus. The complaint, 'I don't have enough faith,' cannot stand, but must become a commitment to seek Jesus Christ himself. If we are in Christ, then we have faith. We can be sure that this faith is adequate, since Christ is complete and perfect.[4]

While other pieces of armor are attached to the body, the shield of faith has to be taken up and actively held in position. A shield is useless unless it is held in position. Faith must be exercised because, *'faith by itself, if it is not accompanied by action, is dead'* (James 2:17).

Imagine that you are standing in the field at Kitty Hawk, North Carolina, where the Wright Brothers are about to launch the their flying machine on its first flight. A small crowd is standing nearby. Everyone has an opinion. Many believe flying is for the birds. Some laugh. Others feel that somewhere, sometime, someone will succeed in defying gravity and fly. A few say they think this contraption will fly.

'What about you,' someone asks, 'Do you believe it will fly? You do? Well, please climb aboard.' Are you still sure? This is the difference between some theoretical belief and true faith. Faith climbs aboard the airplane. *'Now faith is being sure of what we hope for and certain of what we do not see'* (Hebrews 11:1). Faith involves action – it takes risks.

This characteristic of faith – its activity – makes it effective against unbelief. Mental assent and theoretical belief can exist comfortably with passivity, doubt and unbelief. They may even enjoy one another! But faith has no room for them. They are nothing but flimsy, worthless counterfeits.

> *'But when he asks, he must believe and not doubt, because he who doubts is like a wave of the sea, blown and tossed by the wind. That man should not think he will receive anything from the Lord; he is a double-minded man, unstable in all he does.'* (James 1:6–8)

Faith is active. Held in position, the shield of faith will extinguish all the flaming arrows of the enemy, repelling his attack. Our faith will be constantly tested and tried, so it can become strong, pure and full grown.[5] God assures us that we *'through faith are shielded by God's power until the coming of the salvation that is ready to be revealed in the last time'* (1 Peter 1:5). The flaming arrows of the evil one are no threat to genuine faith. The shield of faith is designed to extinguish them. As gold is refined in fire, so faith is refined, purified and proved true by trials (1 Peter 1:6–7). After all, a shield is made for battle.

> *'You give me your shield of victory,*
> *and your right hand sustains me;*
> *you stoop down to make me great.*
> *You broaden the path beneath me,*
> *so that my ankles do not turn.'* (Psalm 18:35–36)

Thank you, Lord, for your gift of faith in Christ Jesus, my shield of victory (1 John 5:4–5). I rejoice that your shield of faith is not some cardboard substitute, but is genuine and able to protect me from the enemy's counterfeit 'faiths'. Lord, I even rejoice in the trials that test my faith, that it may be refined, proved genuine and *'result in praise, glory,*

and honor when Jesus Christ is revealed' (1 Peter
1:6–8).

6. The Helmet of Salvation

'O Sovereign LORD, my strong deliverer,
who shields my head in the day of battle.'

(Psalm 140:7)

The helmet of salvation is protection for our heads – our
minds, perceptions, and thoughts. How crucial. Our
thoughts largely determine our attitudes. Our attitudes
influence our wills, and our wills determine our actions.
No matter how fit our bodies, if our minds are overrun, we
may be rendered useless to God.

Satan is no gentleman. He respects no boundaries, is
devoid of all restraint and is thoroughly evil. He is capable
of interjecting his thoughts into our minds. He seeks to
invade our minds and to make us think his thoughts. He
aims to break down the borders of our minds and gain a
foothold. From there he will try to overrun the whole
person. He seeks to corrupt, distort, and even obliterate
our personalities to manifest his own. Satan seeks to
degrade and humiliate us in order to mock God who
created us in his own image. God loves us and wants us to
reflect his glory. God loves us so much he sent his Son to
rescue us from corruption, including corrupt thinking, by
giving us new life in Jesus Christ.

Jesus Christ himself is our salvation, our Savior who
rescues us from the enemy. He delivers us from corrupt
and distorted thinking by giving us his own mind. *'But we
have the mind of Christ'* (1 Corinthians 2:16). As we learn
the battlefield disciplines of Spirit-controlled living,
constantly giving bodies to God in worship, he transforms
our minds so that we can perceive, understand and
perform his will (Romans 12:1–2).

While Satan may be able to interject thoughts into our minds, we can choose whether or not to entertain them. Any thought may be our own, from the Holy Spirit, or from Satan. An intimate personal relationship with God and a disciplined thought life are foundational to discerning the source of our thoughts. A commitment to holiness in the secret kingdom of our thoughts will keep us vigilant. If we habitually indulge in daydreaming, fantasies, unclean thoughts or careless thinking, we cannot at the same time securely wear God's helmet of salvation. A mind filled with images of worldly pleasures and sins, and feeding on pornography, violence or gossip cannot very well have the mind of Christ. We must choose, and we must take positive action. The things that pollute our minds have to go.

God's helmet of salvation also protects us from doubt. The basis of our assurance is the salvation God freely gives us in Christ Jesus. When Paul wrote his second letter to Timothy, he was a prisoner, arrested for preaching the gospel (2 Timothy 1:8, 16). At his first hearing, no one had shown up to support him (2 Timothy 4:16). Paul might have wondered if he had made some sort of mistake. He could have asked, 'Where is the victory of Jesus now? What has gone wrong? I trusted in Jesus and look where it has gotten me.'

But this is not what we hear from Paul. Although he was suffering, lonely, and disappointed, the assurance of God's salvation rings out from one end of the letter to the other. Paul was certain God would finish what he had started. '. . . *I know whom I have believed and am convinced that he is able to guard what I have entrusted to him for that day*' (2 Timothy 1:12). He was confident that God would deliver him safely to heaven. '*The Lord will rescue me from every evil attack and will bring me safely to his heavenly kingdom. To him be glory for ever and ever*' (2 Timothy 4:18).

Today many of us have little assurance of God's salvation. We are not completely certain God can or will save us. When failure comes or when we are assailed by doubts caused by man's intellectual arguments, our confidence is shaken. How we need God's helmet of salvation so that we can rest securely in all he has promised us.

In Joe's first battle, he was nearly overwhelmed with fear. All he had learned flew right out of his mind as fear rushed in. He felt mentally paralyzed. It was all he could do just to stand his ground. The noise and confusion were tremendous. He wanted to run. All he could remember was what had been drilled into him. He could almost hear the drill sergeant's voice barking orders and encouragement. This discipline and practice enabled Joe to make the right responses even in the midst of overwhelming and threatening circumstances. He was surprised to find that he could do his assigned job competently and without hesitation.

Battle is confusing and disorienting. Visibility may be obscured by terrain, weather, darkness or the enemy. So it is with the spiritual battle. The person disciplined by God's word and prayer will be able to stand firmly in the midst of the spiritual noise and confusion of battle. All those daily times with God – reading his word, committing it to memory, listening to his voice, and speaking with him – are the foundations of the discipline and training that protect our minds and make us able to stand.

Though we may feel afraid, we need not give way to fear. *'For God did not give us a spirit of timidity, but a spirit of power, of love and of self-discipline'* (2 Timothy 1:7).

Though we may experience confusion, it need not overwhelm us. *'For God is not a God of disorder but of peace'* (1 Corinthians 14:33). (*'For God is not the author of confusion, but of peace ... '*) (KJV).

We all want to be able to stand our ground in battle. Our minds themselves are a battleground. Shielded by God's powerful salvation, prepared for action by daily training and discipline, we can be well equipped to *'take captive every thought to make it obedient to Christ'* (2 Corinthians 10:5).

> *'Therefore, prepare your minds for action; be self-controlled; set your hope fully on the grace to be given you when Jesus Christ is revealed. As obedient children, do not conform to the evil desires you had when you lived in ignorance. But just as he who called you is holy, so be holy in all you do; for it is written: "Be holy, because I am holy."'*   (1 Peter 1:13–16)

Father God, I accept your helmet of salvation. Shield and protect my mind from all the assaults of the enemy. May your grace and mercy penetrate into every area of my mind. Cleanse my mind and make me holy. Rescue me from doubt and from all *'hollow and deceptive philosophy which depends on human tradition and the basic principles of this world rather than on Christ'* (Colossians 2:8). Please give me assurance of your salvation. Help me to meditate on and obey all your commands. Fill my mind with your word and make your thoughts my thoughts. Finally, Lord, *'whatever is true, whatever is noble, whatever is right, whatever is pure, whatever is lovely, whatever is admirable – if anything is excellent or praiseworthy – [help me to] think about such things'* (Philippians 4:8).

7. The Sword of the Spirit Which is the Word of God

> *'You are my refuge and my shield;*
>   *I have put my hope in your word.'*
>
>   (Psalm 119:114)

The Sword of the Spirit, the word of God, is one of our two most powerful weapons. Here we will look at it as a defensive weapon. Let us look at Satan's temptation of Jesus in Matthew 4:1–11 and see how Jesus defended himself. As we look at the temptations Jesus faced, we will recognize them as ones we also face.

Jesus had been baptized in water and the Holy Spirit had come upon him, anointing him. His ministry was launched. Anyone who has been anointed and empowered by the Holy Spirit can be sure that he, like Jesus, will be tested. How will he use God's power?

Temptation No. 1 – Will you use God's power to meet your own needs?

Jesus was hungry. This was not the polite hunger of missing a few meals, but the hunger of starvation brought on by forty days of fasting. The temptation goes something like this: 'Turn the stones into bread! Come on? You're a king's kid – you deserve it! This is a legitimate need – there's nothing wrong with eating.'

Jesus recognized the real issue. His defense was a simple declaration from God's word: *'It is written: "Man does not live on bread alone, but on every word that comes from the mouth of God."'* Jesus' life was not in bread – it is in God himself. He chose to trust God to provide what he required. He refused to manipulate God's power to meet his own needs. Jesus would use God's power only in obedience to God's command.

What about us? Will we use God's power to enrich ourselves or to meet our needs, even legitimate ones? Do we look at God's power as a personal seal of approval? Do we expect a financial or some other benefit as the result of our ministry? Let us take great care not to use God's power to meet our own needs. Let us humbly ask him to provide.

**Temptation No. 2 – Will you use God's power to
validate your ministry or prove your identity?**
Satan stood Jesus on the highest point of the temple and
challenged him, ' *"If you are the Son of God,"* he said,
*"throw yourself down. For it is written: 'He will command
his angels concerning you, and they will lift you up in their
hands, so that you will not strike your foot against a
stone'"* ' (Matthew 4:6). Satan does not hesitate to quote
God's word. He knows it well and he will twist and distort
it to suit his purpose.

'Come on! Show everyone who you are. You are God's
anointed one, so prove it. What are you waiting for? You
want everyone to believe, don't you? If you don't just step
out in faith, then it's obvious that you don't really believe
in yourself. How can you expect others to believe? Come
on, prove it!'

But Jesus was not out to 'prove' anything. He lived in
submission and obedience to the Father. He would not
step outside God's will to prove anything. Jesus answered,
*'It is also written: "Do not put the Lord your God to the
test"* ' (Matthew 4:7).

Each of us who lays hand to this sword will do well to
remember God's word is the sword of the Spirit. It is alive
and powerful. The Holy Spirit may wield his sword
through us, but it is **his** sword.

Do not think that you can take hold of God's word to
test it and prove it. That is Satan's tactic. If Jesus could not
put God's word to the test, how can we? Yet we Christians
sometimes try to do this in prayer. We read a verse in the
Bible and claim it for our situation. We declare that we will
stand on God's word and prove it true. In a sense we try
to twist God's arm up behind his back. 'God will answer,'
we say. 'He has to; it's his word.' I believe this is a wrong
use of God's word. Is this what Peter had in mind when he

referred to people who distort scripture to their own destruction (2 Peter 3:16)?

If we let him, however, God will use his word to test and prove us. There is an interesting phrase in Psalm 105 about Joseph, '... *sold as a slave. They bruised his feet with shackles, his neck was put in irons, till what he foretold came to pass, till the word of the Lord proved him true*' (verses 17–19). God used his word to prove and refine Joseph. We are not to test God's word. That has already been done because God declares that '... *the words of the* LORD *are flawless, like silver refined in a furnace of clay, purified seven times*' (Psalm 12:6). While God's word does not need further testing, we do.

Jesus himself submitted to God's word. He did what it said. Ten times in the Gospel of Matthew we read that the events of Jesus' life had '*all taken place that the writings of the prophets might be fulfilled*' (Matthew 26:56).[7] Jesus submitted himself God's word, and so must we.

Temptation No. 3 – Will you try to do the work of God outside the will of God? Will you avoid the cross?

Finally Satan showed Jesus all the kingdoms of this world. 'Look, Jesus! You can have them all right now. I'll give them to you. Just worship me. Such a small thing – no one needs to know. All this business about going to the cross is so unnecessary! You can accomplish your goal without dying. Why throw your life away? What a waste. Don't be foolish!'

Of course, this was a deadly trap like the others. Not even God incarnate could do God's work outside of God's will. It was God's will that Jesus suffer and die as a sacrifice for our sin (Isaiah 53:10). '*Jesus said to him, "Away from me, Satan! For it is written: Worship the Lord your God, and serve him only"*' (Matthew 4:10).

Worshiping and serving God mean sacrifice and crucified lives (Romans 12:1–2). There can be no compromise. Jesus knew this and taught it clearly. *'He then began to teach them that the Son of Man must suffer many things and be rejected by the elders, chief priests and teachers of the law, and that he must be killed and after three days rise again'* (Mark 8:31).

This world, your flesh and the devil will all tell you that the cross is unnecessary. You may even hear their voices in church. They may tell you, 'Jesus suffered and died for us so that we don't have to go to the cross.' But that is not what Jesus taught. After Jesus explained he was going to die in Mark 8:31, Peter took him aside and told him not to go to the cross. Jesus recognized the voice as Satan's and rebuked him. *'If anyone would come after me,'* he continued, *'he must deny himself and take up his cross and follow me. For whoever wants to save his life will lose it, but whoever loses his life for me and for the gospel will save it'* (Mark 8:34–35).

Jesus also said, *'The hour has come for the Son of Man to be glorified. I tell you the truth, unless a kernel of wheat falls to the ground and dies, it remains only a single seed. But if it dies, it produces many seeds. The man who loves his life will lose it, while the man who hates his life in this world will keep it for eternal life. Whoever serves me must follow me; and where I am, my servant also will be. My Father will honor the one who serves me'* (John 12:23–26). Anyone who follows Jesus, follows him to the cross.

We will face the same temptations Christ did. We belong to him. We share his life, and we also share his enemies (John 15:18–20). Jesus Christ, the sinless and perfect Son of God, defended himself against Satan's attacks exclusively by declaring Scripture. Three times Satan tempted him and three times he answered, *'It is written.'* What better defense could we have than that which Jesus himself used? And if Christ defended himself this way, how much more we need to do so.

'And the words of the LORD are flawless, like silver refined in a furnace of clay, purified seven times' (Psalm 12:6). God's word is a perfect, faultless defense. Let us hide God's word in our hearts. Let us ask God to engrave his commands on our hearts. May the Lord, by his Spirit, enable us to wield the sword of the Spirit, the Word of God.

> Heavenly Father, thank you for your perfect word. I praise you that your word is a powerful and perfect defense against all the attacks, schemes and arguments of Satan. Give me a hunger for your word that it may be my food – morning, noon and night. Protect me from the evil one. Give me that living and active word which, by your Spirit, can defend and rescue me when I am tempted. I belong to you, Lord Jesus. Keep and defend me, perfect Word of God. Amen.

Notes

1. *Webster's New World Dictionary of the American Language*, Second College Edition. World Publishing Co., 1980, p. 76.
2. For further study, see also 1 Thessalonians 5:4–11.
3. See also, Matthew 24:44–51.
4. See also, Genesis 15:1, 6.
5. See also, Matthew 17:17–21.
6. Some of these ideas about Jesus' temptation come from *Tried and Transfigured*, by Leonard Ravenhill. Bethany House Publishers, Minneapolis, 1963.
7. Matthew 1:21, 2:15 & 23, 4:14, 8:17, 12:17, 13:35, 21:4, 26:56, 27:35. See also Luke 24:44.

Chapter 3

Praying in the Spirit

'And pray in the Spirit on all occasions with all kinds of prayers and requests.'   (Ephesians 6:18)

What does it mean to 'pray in the Spirit'? Some people have told me that praying in the Spirit is automatic because the Holy Spirit is in all Christians. But if that is true, why is it so hard to pray? Why do we struggle with prayerlessness? Why are many prayers unanswered? Others have told me that praying in the Spirit means praying in tongues. But this answer does not seem satisfactory. Paul, who told us to *'pray in the Spirit on all occasions,'* also said, *'For if I pray in a tongue, my spirit prays, but my mind is unfruitful. So what shall I do? I will pray with my spirit, but I will also pray with my mind . . . '* (1 Corinthians 14:14–15). So, praying with one's spirit and praying with one's mind must be two different occasions. Praying **with** one's spirit, that is, praying in tongues, and praying **in** the Spirit are not necessarily the same thing. So, what is praying in the Spirit?

Praying in the Spirit is praying under the direction of and in harmony with the Holy Spirit, in the name of Jesus Christ, and according to the will of God the Father. It is Spirit-led prayer. It is praying God's will be done and knowing what his will is. When we pray in the Spirit we have the leading of the Holy Spirit to pray God's will. We enjoy the assurance that our prayers have been answered. We often get what we ask for. *'This is the confidence that we have in approaching God: that if we ask anything according to his will, he hears us. And if we know that he hears us – whatever we ask – we know that we have what we asked of him'* (1 John 5:14–15).

Why do we need to pray in the Spirit? Quite simply, the Bible tells us that we do not know how to pray. Romans 8:6–8 explains that unless we are controlled by the Holy Spirit, we will be controlled by our sinful nature. If we are controlled by our sinful nature, we cannot please God. In verses Romans 8:26–27 Paul says, *'In the same way, the Spirit helps us in our weakness. We do not know what we ought to pray, but the Spirit himself intercedes for us with groans that words cannot express. And he who searches our hearts knows the mind of the Spirit, because the Spirit intercedes for the saints in accordance with God's will.'* God answers Spirit-led prayers because they are in accord with God's will and desire.

Praying in the Spirit is not difficult and can be learned. The Spirit himself is quite willing to teach and lead us (John 14:26, 16:13–15). We need to learn to listen to him and follow his direction. We can have confidence that God will indeed lead us and that he will not lead us astray.

> *'So I say to you: Ask and it will be given to you; seek and you will find; knock and the door will be opened to you. For everyone who asks receives; he who seeks finds; and to him who knocks, the door will be opened.*
>
> *Which of you fathers, if your son asks for a fish, will give him a snake instead? Or if he asks for an egg, will give him a scorpion? If you then, though you are evil, know how to give good gifts to your children, how much*

*more will your Father in heaven give the Holy Spirit
to those who ask him!'* (Luke 11:9–13)

Our Battle Position – Rest

*'Let the beloved of the LORD rest secure in him,
  for he shields him all day long,
  and the one the LORD loves rests between his
    shoulders.'* (Deuteronomy 33:12)

We are **in** Christ Jesus, and he means for us to be
resting in intimate fellowship with him – resting between
his shoulders, close against the Lord's breast like John
(John 13:23, 25). Resting in Christ, we are shielded,
protected and safe in his arms. We also can hear our
Lord's heartbeat and detect even his whisper. This is our
battle position and it is here that we can pray in the Spirit.
Here also we will experience power in prayer.

But not many of us are willing to pray from a position of
rest. Most of us are a little like one of Joe's fellow soldiers,
Carl. He was very 'gung ho', anxious for any chance to go
out and stomp the enemy. He hated training exercises,
maneuvers and disciplined marches. He was the first to
volunteer for any dangerous assignment. Carl was so
anxious to get out there and attack the enemy that he often
failed to listen and obey orders. One day his failure to heed
orders resulted in his being seriously wounded. But Carl
was proud of his wounds. He remained oblivious to the fact
that they were the result of his failure to obey orders and
function as a team member. He would need healing, rest
and retraining before he would be ready for action again.

Some Christians are like Carl. Excited about spiritual
warfare, yet only dimly aware of enemy tactics, they
move ahead independently. They are anxious to take
on all the spiritual forces of wickedness in high places

single-handedly. They think spiritual warfare is for 'Rambos' while it is really for God's little sheep. They are frequently wounded.

We are naturally problem-oriented. We are very good at seeing what is wrong, and we want to fix it. So we pray problem-oriented, 'fix-it' prayers. However, prayer led by the Holy Spirit and prayer generated from focusing on the problem are not the same thing. To get free from ourselves and our problem-oriented point of view, we need to learn to enter into the Lord's rest. Beginning in this place of rest, close to the Lord's heart and sensitive to his voice, we can be easily led by the Holy Spirit.

Beverly was a gifted Christian worker. She became concerned about two co-workers when she realized they were sexually involved with one another. Beverly did not expose their secret, but zeroed-in on the problem in prayer. She looked for an opportunity to speak to them or to get them some help, but it did not happen. Meanwhile, others covered up for the wayward couple. Beverly had stumbled upon a nasty little stronghold of secrets and sin that involved a number of people, all of whom were covering up for each other. Feeling isolated and embattled, Beverly nevertheless continued to pray.

Only two months later, Beverly was surprised to find herself involved in a similar relationship. Despite a lot of pressure to keep it secret, Beverly chose to walk in the light. She informed her boyfriend that she would not continue. She met with her leaders to seek their help and counsel. A wounded Beverly escaped the enemy's deadly trap. Her boyfriend, initially angry and uncooperative, changed his mind. Later he said he was thankful and relieved. We need to learn three things about spiritual warfare that Beverly learned the hard way.

1. We need to learn to identify strongholds and be cautious in dealing with them. When we pray for

others, we oppose Satan. Beverly, in praying for her co-workers, disturbed a stronghold and the enemy went on the offensive. Beverly was isolated, vulnerable and unprepared. There are different kinds of strongholds, but I suspect one when a situation features a combination of sin and conspiracy. We need to take up a position of rest in the Lord and follow his lead. Perhaps the Lord will not want us to do anything. Often, our strategy will involve binding the strong man and then disassembling the stronghold, freeing its captives (Matthew 12:29; Mark 3:27; Luke 11:21).

2. The battle is not just 'out there'. We need to be ready to live and walk in what we pray. If we, like Beverly, pray for someone bound in sexual immorality, we may soon find ourselves tempted in a similar way. We need to be aware of our own vulnerabilities and weaknesses. We need to realize that our prayer battle may become very personal. The battle line we perceived as 'out there' may soon run down the center of our own lives. We should never consider ourselves immune to weakness and sin. *'So, if you think you are standing firm, be careful that you don't fall!'* (1 Corinthians 10:12).

3. Beverly did not understand our paradoxical battle position – rest. She did not understand that she needed protection in Christ Jesus. She did not know how to experience the Holy Spirit's leading in prayer. She saw a problem that needed solving. She did not know that she needed to abide, remain and 'rest' in him, going forward only as he directed.

Entering into God's Rest

What exactly is God's rest? We cannot very well sit around all day and do nothing. How do we rest?

Rest is God's idea. He instituted the Sabbath at

creation. Our English word Sabbath comes from a Hebrew word that simply means to rest.[1] God completed all the work of creation in six days and on the seventh he rested, blessing the seventh day and making it holy (Genesis 2:2–3). After God rescued the children of Israel from the slavery of Egypt, he commanded them to rest on the Sabbath (Exodus 20:8–11).

While the children of Israel wandered in the wilderness, God miraculously provided for them daily food in the form of manna which appeared on the ground each morning as the dew dried. It could be made into bread or boiled to make cereal (Exodus 16:14–15). They were to collect a certain amount for each person (Exodus 16:16). But manna was strange stuff. *'The Israelites did as they were told; some gathered much, some little. And when they measured it by the omer, he who gathered much did not have too much, and he who gathered little did not have too little. Each one gathered as much as he needed'* (Exodus 16:17–18). No leftovers were to be kept. When people did try to keep it, it got full of maggots and stank (Exodus 16:19–20). However, on the sixth day the people were to gather twice as much and prepare it, since they were not to work on the Sabbath. When they kept it overnight for the Sabbath this remarkable food did not spoil and they had food to eat on their day of rest (Exodus 16:22–30).

What marvelous provision God gave his people. He even provided for them while they rested. But the people found it difficult to rest. Some people tried to keep the manna overnight and some tried to gather it on the Sabbath. God was angry at their refusal to enter into the rest he had provided for them (Exodus 16:20, 27–28).

Hebrews 3:7–4:16 discusses God's rest in detail. Even a casual reading reveals that God's people were not able to enter into his rest because of unbelief (Hebrews 3:19). God's people were to trust him for their needs one day at a time. To rest on the Sabbath, the people had to trust God to provide for both the sixth and seventh days. They had to believe that the food left over would be wholesome and unspoiled. Failure to act in faith resulted in struggling to provide for themselves, in being confronted with the stinking results of their unbelief and in going hungry.

Resting was difficult. Perhaps they, like us, wanted to be practical, prepared for the future with something laid aside in case God failed to provide. They wanted to work rather than trust.

'There remains, then, a Sabbath-rest for the people of God; for anyone who enters God's rest also rests from his own work, just as God did from his' (Hebrews 4:9–10). To enter God's rest, we must quit striving and rest from our own work. God is our protection and our provision. (I am not saying that all Christians should resign from their jobs to 'live by faith'. Paul left no doubt about that point when he wrote to the Christians in Thessalonica (2 Thessalonians 3:6–12). Each of us is called to live by faith whether employed or not. We can certainly enter into God's rest while fully employed. The kind of work I am talking about is the attitude of self-effort and self-provision to which we humans are so prone.)

Relating God's rest to praying in the Spirit, we must cease praying our own prayers. We must pray from a place of rest in Christ, otherwise our prayers will be filled with our own fruitless efforts. They will not be based on God's will and the breath of God's Spirit will not be in them. However, if we dare to trust him and to enter into his rest, we will enjoy refreshment as well as God's direction, fellowship and power to pray in the Spirit.

'I am the vine; you are the branches. If a man remains in me and I in him, he will bear much fruit; apart from me you can do nothing' (John 15:5). Apart from him we cannot pray in the Spirit. Apart from him we can do nothing. A

branch does not struggle to produce fruit. The fruit grows simply because the life of the vine flows through the branch. The branch does not have to do anything except remain in the vine. This is the only basic thing we must do to pray in the Spirit – we must simply rest in Christ Jesus.

> *'My soul finds rest in God alone;*
>   *my salvation comes from him.*
> *He alone is my rock and my salvation;*
>   *he is my fortress, I will never be shaken ...*
> *Find rest, O my soul, in God alone;*
>   *my hope comes from him.*
> *He alone is my rock and my salvation;*
>   *he is my fortress, I will not be shaken.*
> *My salvation and my honor depend on God;*
>   *he is my mighty rock, my refuge.*
> *Trust in him at all times, O people;*
>   *pour out your hearts to him,*
>   *for God is our refuge.'*   (Psalm 62:1-2, 5-8)

Not only are we to rest in God, but also God wants to rest in us. If we remain in him and he in us, we will be amply supplied and bear much fruit.

> *'For the LORD has chosen Zion,*
>   *he has desired it for his dwelling:*
> *"This is my resting place for ever and ever;*
>   *here will I sit enthroned, for I have desired it –*
> *I will bless her with abundant provisions;*
>   *her poor will I satisfy with food.*
> *I will clothe her priests with salvation,*
>   *and her saints will ever sing for joy."'*
>   (Psalm 132:13-16)

I trust in you, O Lord. Help me to make you my refuge. May you alone be my resting place. Help me to cease from the striving of my own work, ideas, plans and purposes. Give me, instead, your thoughts, plans and purposes.

I trust you to keep me safe and to enable me to pray according to your will as I rest in you. Cause me to hear your gentle whispers and to continually be close to you, able to hear your heartbeat and move as one with you. Enable me to pray 'may your will be done' and to know what your will is. Teach me to pray in the Spirit.

Help me to abide and rest in you and to be fruitful for you. As I find my rest in you, may you also find in me a resting place and enjoy your fruit.[2]

A Man Under Authority

'But say the word, and my servant will be healed. For I myself am a man under authority, with soldiers under me. I tell this one, "Go," and he goes; and that one, "Come," and he comes. I say to my servant, "Do this," and he does it.'

When Jesus heard this, he was amazed at him, and turning to the crowd following him, he said, "I tell you, I have not found such great faith even in Israel."'

(Luke 7:7–9)

Like our friend Joe, this centurion was an army man. A centurion commanded one hundred men. He did so under the authority of his commanding officer. He knew how to submit to authority, and he knew how to exercise it. He understood that his authority depended upon his obedience to his commander.

Our army analogy breaks down here, because the church of Jesus Christ is not a military organization. We are not called to the blind obedience of an infantryman. The church is the body of Christ, and we are members of his body. Each member needs to be in the right place doing what God has called him to do. We must respect and honor those God has placed in leadership positions. We must not be rebellious. For a body to be healthy and functioning as designed, the members of the body must be at peace with one another and work together as one.

Jesus Christ has given us tremendous authority. However, our ability to exercise this authority depends in a large measure on how we submit ourselves to God's authority. Are we part of the local church? Do we have a regular involvement? What is our attitude towards the church leaders, towards other members? Do we have any strained or broken relationships? We can exercise Christ's authority only to the extent that we submit ourselves under his authority. Yielded to Jesus Christ, and submitting ourselves as members of his body, we can exercise Christ's authority. If we refuse to be related with Christ in his body, or if we are not living in peace with each other, we effectively take ourselves out of the 'chain of command'. If we fail to submit to Christ's authority, we cannot possibly exercise it.

Humility

> 'This is the one I esteem:
>   he who is humble and contrite in spirit,
>   and trembles at my word.'   (Isaiah 66:2b)

What quality of character is more misunderstood, elusive and maligned than humility? Like a soap bubble that bursts at the slightest touch, humility evaporates with the first glimmer of its self-consciousness. How can we discuss something so elusive?

While men give lip-service to the virtue of humility, in

our world today true humility is despised. The humble, the meek are called weak, non-assertive, spineless – 'door mats'. The world advises, 'You have to stick up for yourself or people will walk all over you. If you don't look out for number one, no one else will.'

But the Lord esteems the humble (Isaiah 66:2b), gives the humble grace (1 Peter 5:6), and declares that the meek will inherit the earth (Matthew 5:5). Jesus says he himself is humble and meek and he invites us to share his yoke (Matthew 11:29–30). How different is the kingdom where Jesus Christ reigns from the kingdoms of this world! What the world despises, heaven esteems. What the world treasures is worthless in heaven (Luke 16:15; Matthew 6:19–21, 23:10–12; Luke 12:33–34).

We are either citizens of the kingdom of heaven or citizens of the kingdom of this world. We must claim one and renounce the other. We cannot hold dual citizenship. God calls us to pledge our allegiance to him alone. The choice is ours.

When it comes to prayer and intercession, the Bible displays two outstanding examples of humility – Moses and Jesus.

1. Moses – the Face-Down Leader

> *'Now Moses was a very humble man, more humble than anyone else on the face of the earth.'*
>
> (Numbers 12:3)

What an extraordinary testimony. After escaping the infanticide decreed by Pharaoh, Moses was raised under Pharaoh's nose by Pharaoh's own daughter, heir to all the privileges of Egypt. Attempting to act as a champion for his own people, Moses killed an Egyptian and ended up fleeing for his life. He spent the next forty years hiding out, herding sheep in the desert. He was eighty years old when God sent him to confront Pharaoh and rescue his people.

Through Moses God worked spectacular miracles. Moses confronted Pharaoh, rescued Israel, led an entire nation, taught God's commands, interpreted God's laws to the people, oversaw law and order, directed daily and religious life and kept faithful records. Moses' achievements during these forty years, from age eighty to one hundred twenty were remarkable by any standards.

Moses repeatedly faced opposition and rebellion from dissatisfied, grumbling people who refused to follow. The way Moses handled opposition does not appear in management training materials, leadership manuals, or books on self-assertion.

Two elements of Moses' leadership particularly stand out, and they are interrelated – intercession and humility. Moses faithfully stood in the gap and interceded for the people before God. He pleaded for mercy and asked forgiveness for their sin. He identified with those for whom he interceded and was willing to lay down his life for them, *'So Moses went back to the Lord and said, "O what a great sin these people have committed! They have made themselves gods of gold. But now, please forgive their sin – but if not, then blot me out of the book you have written"'* (Exodus 32:31-32). That is intercession. God's commands and plans came first, the needs of others next and Moses' own needs last.

When his authority was challenged, Moses' responded, *'Who are we* [Moses and Aaron], *that you should grumble against us? . . . Who are we? You are not grumbling against us, but against the Lord'* (Exodus 16:7-8). Moses was willing to be a nobody. He was unconcerned about his position and public image. He had no desire to assert himself. He did care a great deal about God's plans and people.

When his authority was challenged, such was the heart of this intercessor and leader, that he *'fell face down in front of the whole Israelite assembly gathered there'* (Numbers 14:5). So great was his fear of God and his humility that Moses repeatedly fell face down in front of those who opposed him to intercede for them. What a contrast to the manipulative and aggressive training today's image-conscious leaders receive.

We long to see the power of God released in our lives and the lives of those for whom we pray. Are we willing to forsake our own power so we will be free to receive God's power? Moses was.

2. Jesus – Humbled Himself and Became Obedient to Death

> *'Do nothing out of selfish ambition or vain conceit, but in humility consider others better than yourselves. Each of you should look not only to your own interests, but also to the interests of others. Your attitude should be the same as that of Christ Jesus: Who, being in very nature God, did not consider equality with God something to be grasped, but made himself nothing, taking the very nature of a servant, being made in human likeness.*
>
> *And being found in appearance as a man, he humbled himself and became obedient to death – even death on a cross! Therefore God exalted him to the highest place and gave him the name that is above every name, that at the name of Jesus every knee should bow, in heaven and on earth and under the earth, and every tongue confess that Jesus Christ is Lord, to the glory of God the Father.'*
>
> (Philippians 2:3–11)

Jesus Christ, God, the creator and Lord of all *'made*

himself nothing.' He was born a man. He became a servant. Then he went even further – *'he humbled himself and became obedient to death – even death on a cross'* (Philippians 2:8).

The reason Jesus has been exalted to the highest place and has been given the greatest name and all authority and power is because of his humility – because he willingly chose the lowest place. Jesus the intercessor, exalted at God's right hand, is the same Jesus who humbled himself to death. He extends us the invitation to follow him, to humble ourselves. It is an invitation we cannot refuse, *'For everyone who exalts himself will be humbled, and he who humbles himself will be exalted'* (Luke 18:14). We can humble ourselves or God will do it for us, but humility we must have. Choosing humility means choosing the attitude of Jesus Christ. Jesus chose humility and those of us who follow him must also choose to humble themselves.

Humility is the intercessor's pathway. Humility is our access to God's throne of grace because *'God opposes the proud, but gives grace to the humble'* (James 4:6). Humility provides not only a right relationship with God, but also with others. Humility provides a right position for intercession. Humility gives us a higher opinion of others than of ourselves. We are called to serve and care for others without an eye to our own gain (Philippians 2:3-4).

Humility puts others first, falls face down and pleads before God's throne of grace for those who oppose, reject or mistreat. Humility is not conscious of itself – it has eyes only for God's will and others' good. *'All of you, clothe yourselves with humility toward one another ... Humble yourselves, therefore, under God's mighty hand, that he may lift you up in due time'* (1 Peter 5:5, 6).

When we choose humility, we do not exalt ourselves, our perceptions, opinions or ideas. Humility enables us to share God's perceptions and to pray in the Spirit.

Unhindered by selfish ambition or vain conceit, we will receive grace to pray according to God's will with perfect freedom and full authority.

Submission and Resistance

> *'Submit yourselves, then, to God. Resist the devil, and he will flee from you.'*　　　　　　　　(James 4:7)

Choosing friendship with God, rejecting friendship with the world, and humbling ourselves before the Lord form the context of our submission and resistance (James 4:4-10). When we reject friendship with the world and choose to humble ourselves before the Lord, this brings us into submission to God. We will not be rebelling and asserting our own selfish wills. We will also find that we are able to *'submit to one another out of reverence for Christ'* (Ephesians 5:21).

The perfect example of submission is that of the chief intercessor, Jesus Christ. Jesus' submission was such that he could confidently assert that every word he said and everything he did were exactly what God the Father told him to say and do.[3]

Jesus' perfect submission did not come automatically or without cost. Jesus was fully committed to an intimate relationship with his Father. In spite of travel pressures and exhausting ministry demands, Jesus made time for his Father. Apparently Jesus was in the habit of drawing aside to pray, sometimes in the early hours of the morning and sometimes to spend whole nights in prayer.[4]

Most of Jesus' prayers are not recorded – they were private. Jesus both practiced and recommended secret prayer. *'But when you pray, go into your room, close the door and pray to your Father, who is unseen'* (Matthew 6:6.).

From Jesus' prayer in the garden just before his arrest, trial and execution we can see that his submission was not easy and automatic. He urged his disciples, *'Watch and pray so that you will not fall into temptation. The spirit is willing, but the body is weak'* (Matthew 26:41). The flesh is indeed weak. The disciples kept falling asleep.

Jesus' flesh was weak, human flesh, too. Three times Jesus asked his Father if there could be another solution, a way forward without the cross. His struggle was intense (Luke 22:44), but he was able to pray, *'Yet not as I will, but as you will'* (Matthew 26:39). That is submission. The Father's will is first, even unto death.

The one who submits to God also resists the devil – and the devil flees. God commands us to put on God's full armor and to take our stand against the devil's schemes (Ephesians 6:11). As we do this, the devil runs away. He runs because he has already been defeated for *'the reason the Son of God appeared was to destroy the devil's work'* (1 John 3:8). Not only that, but Jesus allows us to share in his victory (1 John 5:4). He is leading us in a triumphal procession, a victory march (2 Corinthians 2:14).

Whom Shall I Fear?

'The LORD is exalted, for he dwells on high;
he will fill Zion with justice and righteousness.
He will be the sure foundation for your times,
a rich store of salvation and wisdom and
knowledge;
the fear of the LORD is the key to this treasure.'
(Isaiah 33:5–6)

Fear is a great crippler. It hinders, paralyzes and binds. If we are afraid, we cannot pray in the Spirit. We will just pray in fear. What are you afraid of? Dogs? Spiders? What about the future or the unknown?

The most common fear among people today is the fear of man. We are bound by fear of what people will think of us and whether they will accept us and approve of us. We want them to like us. We are afraid of disapproval. We are afraid of gossip. We are terrified of rejection. In short, we are terribly afraid of each other.

Because praying in fear prevents praying in the Spirit, and since we want to pray in the Spirit, we need to be set free from the fear of man. God tells us, *'Fear of man will prove to be a snare'* (Proverbs 29:25). The fear of man is a trap which takes us captive, binds and imprisons us. How can we get free? Psalm 25:12–15 gives us the key. This passage describes the man who fears the Lord. Verse 15 says, *'My eyes are ever on the LORD, for only he will release my feet from the snare.'* The fear of man cripples and binds but the fear of the Lord sets us free.

'But wait,' some object. 'We are not supposed to fear the Lord, are we? God is love and perfect love drives out all fear. This fear of the Lord is not for today. That's an Old Testament idea. God does not want us to be afraid of him.' Yes, he does. While fear is powerful, negative and binding, the fear of the Lord is completely different. *'The fear of the Lord is clean, enduring forever'* (Psalm 19:9 KJV). This fear and this fear alone is completely healthy. The fear of the Lord is most surely for every one of us today. From Deuteronomy to Revelation the Bible commands us to fear the Lord.

> *'Love the Lord your God with all your heart and with all your soul and with all your strength … Fear the Lord your God, serve him only and take your oaths in his name.'* (Deuteronomy 6:5, 13)

85

"Then I saw another angel flying in midair, and he had the eternal gospel to proclaim to those who live on the earth – to every nation, tribe, language and people. He said in a loud voice, "Fear God and give him glory, because the hour of his judgment has come. Worship him who made the heavens, the earth, the sea and the springs of water." '   (Revelation 14:6–7)

Those who fear the Lord receive many blessings. The man who fears God will be instructed by the Lord. He will be prosperous. The Lord will confide in him and reveal his covenant to him (Psalm 25:12–15). God's angels will protect him. He will be delivered from all his fears. He will lack nothing (Psalm 34:9–10). He has found the beginning of wisdom and understanding. He will delight in God's commands. He will not fear bad news. He has no fear! He will look in triumph on his enemies. He will receive honor and endure forever (Psalm 111:10–112:10). What blessings, and these are only a selection.

How wonderful – the man who fears the Lord will have no fear. The fear of the Lord delivers from every other fear.

Whatever you fear will be large in your eyes.
May the Lord be large in your eyes.
Choose the fear of the Lord.

Whatever you fear will fill your vision.
May the Lord fill your vision.
Choose the fear of the Lord.

Fear cripples and binds, but the fear of the Lord
    sets you free.
May you be free to fear the Lord.
Choose the fear of the Lord.

The fear of man is a snare but the fear of the Lord
    releases our feet from the snare.
May you be free from the fear of man to fear the
    Lord.
Choose the fear of the Lord.

Father God, I admit to you my weakness. Because of
Jesus' death on the cross, I ask you to forgive me for
the times when I have resisted you and submitted to
Satan. Teach me humility and submission. Lord,
show me how to take my place in the body of
Christ. Help me to live in peace with everyone.
Where my relationships are strained or broken, help
me to put them right. Please teach me submission
that I might learn to exercise your authority.

    Teach me to recognize Satan's tactics and to resist
him. Forgive me for fearing people more than I fear
you. Forgive me for caring more about their opinion
of me than yours. Forgive me for trying to please men
and not seeking what pleases you. Set me free from
the fear of man and teach me the fear of the Lord.
Cause me to want what pleases you, Father, and
teach me to pray in the Spirit.

Recognizing the Enemy

*'For our struggle is not against flesh and blood, but
against the rulers, against the authorities, against the
powers of this dark world and against the spiritual
forces of evil in the heavenly realms.'*

(Ephesians 6:12)

As we go to our knees in prayer, we quickly encounter
enemies. Like Jesus, we experience enemy contact in three
realms: in the heavenly realm – the devil and his minions,
on earth – the world system which is under Satan's

control, and inside ourselves – our own flesh (Romans 7:18). We often need to deal with all of them at the same time. The attractions of the world excite our flesh, stirring up sinful cravings, the lust of our eyes and a heart that boasts against God (1 John 2:15–16). Satan adds his enticements, trying to lead us and others to destruction.

About one thing we must be clear – our enemies are the world, our own flesh, and the devil. **Our enemies are never other people**.

As we pray, interceding and battling, we always pray **for** people, no matter how difficult, offensive or dangerous they may be. If they have hurt us, we forgive them. Even if Satan has taken them captive and is manipulating them for his evil purposes, we must be **for** them in prayer. They may act like our enemies, but God is **for** them. He loves them and so must we. Jesus taught, *'Love your enemies and pray for those who persecute you, that you may be sons of your Father in heaven...'* (Matthew 5:44–45).

Every person is valuable and precious to God. He longs for each one to know him, so he encourages us to pray for every one!

> *'I urge, then, first of all, that requests, prayers and intercession and thanksgiving be made for everyone – for kings and those in authority, that we may live peaceful and quiet lives in all godliness and holiness. This is good, and pleases God our Savior, who wants all men to be saved and come to a knowledge of the truth.'* (1 Timothy 2:1–4)

How many people, do you suppose, have never in their lives been the object of anyone's prayer or intercession? Who do you know or just see in the course of your daily life? Have you ever thought to pray for them? How about the elderly lady who begs for coins near the bus station? Do you ever pray for the people who collect your garbage?

The Weapons of Our Warfare

What about the drug addict or alcoholic in your neighborhood? What about your boss at work, the watchmen at your gate or that classmate no one likes? I wonder what magnificent things would happen if each of us simply got in the habit of praying briefly for everyone we come in contact with. You may be the first person to ever bring these people to God's throne of grace in prayer. You may be the only one who has ever asked for God's blessing, mercy and grace for them. How God loves them and longs to pour out his love upon them. Will you ask for them?

> Father in heaven, I need your help to pray your blessing and grace for the people I regularly meet. Help me pray for those who serve me in public and for those who are rude to me. Forgive me for praying only for myself, that my own way goes smoothly. Change my heart, Lord, and help me to reach out to everyone with the love and grace of God through Christ Jesus.

Flesh or Spirit

> 'Those who live according to the sinful nature have their minds set on what that nature desires; but those who live in accordance with the Spirit have their minds set on what the Spirit desires.' (Romans 8:5)

What moves us to pray? Many of us pass long months of relative prayerlessness – until some emergency arises. Suddenly we are 'moved' and pray fervently – until the crisis passes. This can hardly be called praying in the Spirit. This is emergency praying. To pray in the Spirit, our prayer must be Spirit-initiated and Spirit-led. I am not saying we should not pray in emergencies. We need to pray in every situation (1 Thessalonians 5:17). But in order to learn to pray in the Spirit, we need to examine what moves us to pray.

1. Arson in Their Midst

The distinction between flesh and Spirit-motivated prayer came into focus for me in 1989. My friends in St. Stephen's Society at Hang Fook Camp in Hong Kong were frightened and upset. Almost daily their wooden buildings were being set on fire. Usually the residents spotted and extinguished the fires quickly before much damage was done. But it was a dangerous and frightening situation. Eventually someone would get hurt. One building was burned so badly it had to be torn down. The girls who had lived in it lost all their possessions. Another fire was set in a room next to one where a worker was sleeping. She escaped, choking from smoke and shaking with fear. The fires broke out at all hours of the day and night. Residents of the camp became fearful. Some could not sleep and a few moved elsewhere temporarily. Desperate to discover the arsonist's identity, everyone began to suspect everyone else. The whole place was tense with fear and suspicion.

At home, as I cleared an area to fold our family laundry, I also cleared my heart and mind to pray about the fires. When I began praying I felt as if a gray, featureless wall was directly in front of me. My prayers seemed as flat and gray as that invisible wall. Perhaps I just needed to 'warm up' in prayer. I tried praying about a number of other things. Immediately I sensed the help of the Holy Spirit. Praying came easily, along with a clear sense of God's direction and an assurance of his answers. It was like being carried along in prayer.

'Ah, good,' I thought, 'Now that I'm all warmed up, I'll pray much better about the fires.' But as soon as I changed back to the subject of the fires, there was the same gray, featureless wall. How strange. I tried praying about other things. Again, rather than hindrance, I sensed help from the Lord. But when I returned to the subject of the fires, things again came to a halt.

Baffled, I asked God why was I unable to pray effectively about such an important matter. I gave to God my pressure to 'hear a word from the Lord', the expectations of others and my own desire to look good (fear of man). What else could be in the way?

As far as I know, the arsonist's identity was never discovered. The fires finally stopped, but only after camp residents initiated an exhausting 24-hour full perimeter watch.

God did give me a word that day, but it was not about arson. It was about prayer. I could not hear God's voice and my prayers seemed flat because I was trying to pray in the power of my own flesh. I was being empowered by the urgency of a serious situation, and by fear, distrust and suspicion. I needed to be empowered by the Holy Spirit himself. I needed to fight this battle from a place of rest in Christ Jesus.

To be intercessors, we need to face our own fleshly reactions. We need to come to the Lord and allow him to deal with us until we find a place of rest in him. When we get under pressure or experience an overwhelming need, we get stirred up and feel we must 'do' something. This can take the form of outward activity or be translated into an urgency to pray. Fleshly reaction hinders praying in the Spirit. We need to come to the Lord himself and find our rest and confidence in him. From that place of rest, the Holy Spirit can then direct our prayer and activity. This transition does not happen automatically. As we draw close to the Lord, he will search our hearts and shine his light inside us. He will comfort, heal and correct us. As he does so, he will impart to us his heart and desire. As he removes what is of the flesh, he will give us what is of his Spirit. He will make us able to pray in the Spirit.

2. June 4, 1989 – Hong Kong

Shortly after God began teaching me to distinguish flesh motivated prayer from Spirit-led intercession, Hong Kong was shocked and deeply shaken by the massacre of pro-democracy demonstrators in Tienamen Square in Beijing. The *South China Sunday Morning Post* headlines that morning made me feel dizzy. During the day I felt appalled, exhausted, on the verge of tears and numb. I was certainly not alone.

I needed to pray for our wounded and bleeding neighbor, China, its leaders and its people and the confused, fearful and angry people of Hong Kong. But first I needed to experience the victory of Jesus Christ over my own emotions and reactions. Otherwise, my prayers would be colored and directed by my perceptions, fears and reactions and they would lack the quality of true intercession.

How thankful I was that God had already shown me how to pray. I knew we needed to ask God's help to pray through our feelings and reactions. We needed him to set us free from our own anger, hatred and fear and to enable us to pray in the Spirit.

The first spiritual battle ground is right in our own hearts. We must face our flesh and experience the victory of the Lord Jesus Christ over it. Our weapons in this battle include confession, repentance and the blood of Jesus Christ. Once our own hearts, emotions and motives are dealt with, we are able to intercede in the freedom of the Holy Spirit. How wonderful not to be bound to our fleshly reaction. How wonderful to experience freedom to transcend our flesh and to intercede in the Holy Spirit.

3. No 'Lone Rangers'

When I am in a desperate situation, I pray desperate, scared and helpless prayers. Sometimes I am so overwhelmed I cannot pray at all, let alone find a place of rest in the Lord. Was God saying that praying when I am in desperate need is useless or ineffective? 'Do you mean, Lord, that I can't pray when I'm upset, when my child is desperately ill, when I'm scared, or when I'm angry?' I asked.

No. The Bible makes it very clear that God hears and answers desperate, urgent and importunate prayers (Psalm 61:1-3, 116:1-7; Jonah 2). He cares about our needs and desires. He encourages us to call on him when we are in trouble (Lamentations 2:18-19; Luke 11:4-13, 18:1-8).

> *'The LORD is near to all who call on him,*
> *to all who call on him in truth.*
> *He fulfills the desires of those who fear him;*
> *he hears their cry and saves them.'*
>
> (Psalm 145:18-19)

Also, the Holy Spirit helps us, interceding for us when our heart's cry is beyond words or when we just can not pray (Romans 8:26-27).

God is a wonderful listener. He is a lot like my friend Carol. When I talk to her, I can just be myself. If I am upset about something, she patiently listens to my fussing and complaining. She may offer words of comfort. She does not laugh at me or criticize. When I am done with all that, she will gently direct me to the Lord. She may confront me with my need to forgive someone and she will always call sin, sin. And she prays for me. I know that she intercedes privately for me, seeking to pray God's heart and will for my life. I am sure she often prays things for me that I do not have the wisdom to pray for myself. Sometimes, I can do the same thing for Carol.

God wasn't telling me my prayers were no good. He was telling me that I am a part of the body of Christ. When I am too weak, sick or upset to pray, others hold me up in prayer. I do not have to be a 'Rambo' in prayer. I am part of the body of Christ, and together, under the direction of the Holy Spirit, we intercede and pray for one another. We encourage, bless and build up one another. Intercession and spiritual warfare are not in a vacuum. They are expressions of our life together in Christ Jesus. We are not 'Lone Rangers', but members who fit into a place in the body of Christ designed specially for us. We are each individuals with problems, difficulties and weaknesses. The victory of Jesus Christ over all these is ours collectively, in fellowship with one another.

Recently a couple who teach English in remote north-west China had a real emergency. Lynn, in her fourth month of pregnancy, was haemorrhaging. In China, medical services can be quite primitive. There was nothing they could do medically. A friend, summoned in the middle of the freezing cold night, crawled into bed with the couple and prayed throughout the night. The next day they learned that another friend across town, who knew nothing of their emergency, had been awakened during the night with an urgency to pray. This fellowship in Spirit-led intercession encouraged Lynn and her husband. Lynn's bleeding subsided. Later tests in Hong Kong revealed a placenta-previa. Despite the fact they were facing a surgical delivery and the possibility of dangerous haemorrhages, this couple was confident of the Lord's help and protection. They planned to remain at their teaching post until near time for the baby's arrival. Being surrounded by loving prayer had given them confidence in the Lord. They were conscious of God's support and care through the prayers and intercession of the body of Christ.

A few years ago, my neighbor's lovely 17-year-old daughter, Sarah, was diagnosed with bone cancer. Three out of four biopsies were clearly malignant. My neighbor, Mrs Wu, was devastated. Her blood pressure soared to dangerous levels. She cried, she yelled, and she couldn't stop asking, 'Why, God?' We got together with Mrs Wu to pray. We all intended to pray for Sarah, but we found ourselves first praying for Mrs Wu. Mrs Wu was able to stop screaming 'why?' and to trust in God. God, in his grace, enabled her to surrender her daughter into his hands. She gave him Sarah's life and the cancer.

As the news of Sarah's illness spread, everybody prayed – Mr and Mrs Wu, the Wu's church and many friends, some of whom they had never met. They prayed for Sarah, Mrs Wu and her whole family. They prayed corporately and individually. They listened, blessed and encouraged – and everyone struggled with the pain and the 'why' question.

Soon Sarah was facing major surgery which was certain to leave her disfigured. Her entire lower jaw on one side would have to be removed. The doctors planned to build her a new one with bone grafts from her hip and skull. A week before surgery, she entered the hospital for a final CAT scan. What rejoicing there was when the results came back. The cancer was nowhere to be found! The doctors were dumbfounded. Mrs Wu jumped up and down in the doctor's office and told them Jesus Christ had healed her daughter. She was every bit as full of joy as she had been with distress. Sarah still has scans every six months, but they show only healthy bones. Our rejoicing and thanksgiving knew no bounds. Just as we had participated in this family's pain and shared in their difficulties, so we were part of their rejoicing. The fellowship of prayer and intercession bound us together in Christ Jesus.

Each of us has times when circumstances are overwhelming. We all have bad days and times when our faith is weak. There are times when each one of us desperately needs someone to stand in the gap and intercede for us. And there are times when others need our intercession.

> Father God, I want to pray under the direction of your Holy Spirit. I invite you to search my heart as I pray. I am willing, Lord, to let you deal with my fleshly thoughts and responses through the cross of Jesus Christ. In your mercy, help me to put off the things of the flesh and to choose the things of your Spirit. Teach me to follow the leading of your Holy Spirit and help me to pray and intercede according to your direction.
>
> Lord, please help me to be bold and humble enough to ask others to pray for me when I am struggling. Make me sensitive to the needs of others. Help me to listen without judging and to encourage them to look to you. Help us to come together to your throne of grace. Help me stand with them and intercede on their behalf according to the direction of the Holy Spirit, through Jesus Christ. Amen.

4. Led by the Spirit

'... the Spirit helps us in our weakness ... the Spirit intercedes for the saints in accordance with God's will.'
(Romans 8:26, 27)

How did we learn to pray? Most of us probably learned by listening to others. The first prayers many of us heard were congregational prayers, spoken by one person on behalf of the whole church. We have simply copied what was modeled to us. When we heard someone pray something that impressed us, we tried it out in our own prayers. But what happens when we carry this model into our personal prayer lives? In our personal devotions do our prayers sound more like formal speeches than like a child speaking with his father?

Modeling is an excellent way to teach. Imitating others is a powerful and effective way to learn. But bad models teach just as efficiently as good ones. Since most of us learned to pray by imitating others, it is a good idea to examine our prayer habits. If we are going to learn to pray in the Spirit, then he must be free to lead and direct our praying. Some of our habits may grieve or quench the Holy Spirit.

Do Not Grieve the Holy Spirit

> *'Do not let any unwholesome talk come out of your mouths, but only what is helpful for building others up according to their needs, that it may benefit those who listen. And do not grieve the Holy Spirit of God, with whom you were sealed for the day of redemption. Get rid of all bitterness, rage and anger, brawling and slander, along with every form of malice. Be kind and compassionate to one another, forgiving each other, just as in Christ God forgave you.'*

(Ephesians 4:29-32)

When we harbor sin in our hearts, it invariably comes out of our mouths (Matthew 12:34). Unwholesome talk can come out of our mouths during our prayer and fellowship as well as any other time. This grieves the Holy Spirit.

In group prayer, the most obvious problem area is gossip and slander. Probably all of us have attended a prayer meeting where 'sharing needs' deteriorated into a gossip session. Suddenly someone realized there were only five minutes before the meeting was to end. A perfunctory, hurried prayer was expected to justify all that had gone before. Group members left with an uneasy, dissatisfied feeling, aware of having grieved the Holy Spirit.

Everyone involved in intercession, whether in a group or in secret must learn to keep confidences. Prayer groups will invariably learn of people's private affairs. How the group and each of its members deals with confidentiality is very important. Confidential information must remain in the group. The group should discuss and agree upon how to keep confidentiality. For example, are group members free to discuss the meeting outside the group or tell absent members details of the meeting? Groups need to be reminded often of their confidentiality agreements. I have found it very helpful for members to agree to speak up whenever they sense we are headed for trouble. Accountability belongs to each one. When new members join the group, confidentiality should be thoroughly discussed again. It is a good idea to pray at the end of the meeting, gathering up all 'secrets' and placing them in the Lord's hands, recommiting ourselves to confidentiality.

Our fleshly perceptions, judgments and opinions can pollute the thinking and prayers of the whole group. We must have a deep commitment to speak and pray only what is wholesome, what builds up. This may leave us with little to pray and less to say. Good. That will give the Holy Spirit more opportunity to take the lead. We need to be so zealous to speak and pray only what edifies that we will speak up and correct the group's course when necessary. Most of us are terrified at this prospect, but when people are openly committed to wholesome talk, it is not difficult. A simple, 'I'm not feeling very comfortable with our direction just now. Let's . . . ' is usually sufficient.

Another way we can grieve the Holy Spirit is to violate his confidence. We confide in people we trust. We open ourselves up to those whom we believe will keep what we tell them to themselves. It constantly amazes me that God shares secrets with us. But sharing God's secrets does not place us in some exclusive category. We have not reached some lofty spiritual height because God gives us insight.

Of course, as soon as God does share secrets or give us insight, this is exactly what we begin to think. And how we would like to share our insights with others! We say we want to encourage them, but the secret truth is we want to impress them. This is spiritual pride. In even the smallest quantities it breeds boasting and disconnects us from the body (2 Corinthians 12:1-10; Colossians 2:18-19).

There are a couple of ladies who used to like to inch up alongside me and whisper in my ear. They made oblique references to having some secret revelation which made them superior to the less spiritual. They spoke to me in confidential tones and gave me knowing looks, as if to suggest that they thought I was one of these 'special' people, too. How enticing! Wouldn't it be nice to be part of the 'spiritually élite'?

The 'spiritually élite' may think they are, but in truth, there is no such thing. There is no such thing as a group who receive special revelation not available to the ordinary Christians. Yes, God shares secrets, but he does not play favorites (Romans 2:11; Ephesians 6:9). God freely shares his secrets with anyone who is willing to come close and listen.

In my experience, few things grieve the Holy Spirit more quickly than talking about things that should be secret. Aspects of our individual prayer times are private. As in a marriage, there are some things we simply do not share with anyone else.

Areas we should be cautious about include the details of

what God has led us to pray for an individual or situation (danger of gossip), personal promises or direction the Lord seems to be giving (danger of presumption), revelation related to future events (Daniel 12:4), anything that may be easily misinterpreted, and things which cannot be expressed (2 Corinthians 12:4). Before talking about these things, it is wise to ask the Lord whether we should share them. It is wonderful to be taken into the Lord's confidence. However, when we violate his trust, we grieve him and damage our trust relationship. We need to be just as sensitive to the Lord's direction when we come out of the secret place as when we are in it.

Jesus told his disciples,

> *'But when he, the Spirit of truth, comes, he will guide you into all truth ... He will bring glory to me by taking from what is mine and making it known to you.'* (John 16:13, 14)

> *'When the Counselor comes, whom I will send to you from the Father, the Spirit of truth who goes out from the Father, he will testify about me.'* (John 15:26)

The reason the Holy Spirit reveals God's truth to us is to glorify Jesus Christ. His purpose is to testify about Jesus. The Holy Spirit is wonderfully single-minded. He always glorifies Jesus Christ. His focus is always to exalt Jesus Christ as Lord.

When concentrating on intercession and spiritual warfare, it is very easy to simply lose our focus. When we are concentrating on praying about a particular situation, we quite naturally begin to focus on it. Without our being aware of it, our attention can shift away from the Lord. The more we focus on the situation or problem, the more we lift up the problem instead of lifting up the Lord. This grieves the Holy Spirit.

When we are involved in spiritual warfare, it is easy to begin to focus on the enemy rather than the Lord. Not only does this make it difficult to pray in the Spirit, but it can cause an imbalance in our whole Christian life.

Our focus must always be on Christ Jesus. *'Let us fix our eyes on Jesus, the author and perfecter of our faith...'* (Hebrews 12:2). He is the King of Kings and the Lord of Lords. He is the one who is exalted to the highest place. He is the one who has triumphed over Satan, sin and death. He is our mighty God, our Rock, our Deliverer. He is our life.

Do Not Quench the Holy Spirit

> *'Be joyful always; pray continually; give thanks in all circumstances, for this is God's will for you in Christ Jesus. Do not put out the Spirit's fire; do not treat prophecies with contempt. Test everything. Hold on to the good. Avoid every kind of evil.'*
>
> (1 Thessalonians 5:16–21)

Quenching the Holy Spirit involves not allowing him to express himself. We might be so full of our own ideas and agendas that we squeeze out the Holy Spirit's leading. We might hold back, not allowing the Holy Spirit to move through us. We might even reject his direction because of our own prejudices and opinions.

One practice which can put a damper on the Holy Spirit is what I call 'shopping list' praying. I am not condemning the use of prayer lists; I frequently use them both in private and in groups. The 'shopping list' praying that I am referring to may involve praying mechanically or repetitiously, so our praying becomes a formula. Praying like this seems dangerously similar to occult practice – repeating some formula or 'magic words' to make something happen.

'And when you pray, do not keep babbling like pagans, for they think they will be heard because of their many words. Do not be like them, for your Father knows what you need before you ask him.' (Matthew 6:7–8)

In addition, a flood of verbiage in prayer can easily eclipse God's small, still voice. Rather than listening to God and praying as he directs, we can end up deciding what God should do and telling him to do it as soon as possible. This is more appropriate to ordering groceries than requesting mercy and help from our all-powerful Creator!

Lists are useful in private prayer to help choose a prayer subject. They help us remember who we have been praying for. A private record of how we prayed for a particular person or situation can act as a spring-board for continued intercession and help us recognize God's answers. As I look back over some of my prayer notes, I am amazed at how many prayers God has answered. These are occasions for praise and thanksgiving!

When we fall into habitual patterns of prayer, we are not being led by the Holy Spirit. In small groups, one habitual pattern that hinders the Spirit is the practice of each person praying a complete and independent prayer. Each prayer usually has a formal introduction and closing. These prayers may be decorated with eloquent phrases and often sound very little like the person's ordinary speech. Each person prays as if he is the only person in the room. There is no group interaction. Each person is usually careful to include every request mentioned for prayer, so these prayers tend to be very long.

Many people have expressed to me a sense of frustration and bondage because of this pattern. They feel bored and try to avoid prayer meetings. They tell me that they must be careful to remember each and every request in their prayer, lest someone read a hidden meaning into their omission.

If the group is large, your 'turn' to pray may involve a very long and boring wait. Since the content of each person's prayer is largely predictable, it is difficult to stay alert and interested. Each person prays essentially the same thing as everyone else.

A twist in this pattern involves each person attempting to pray a 'better' prayer than the last one. This is a little less boring, but a sense of one-upsmanship begins to creep around the circle with the chill of spiritual pride. The Holy Spirit cannot move freely here.

It does not have to be like this! We can experience the exciting and dynamic leading of the Holy Spirit in prayer. We need to stop clinging to the predictability of our habits (Matthew 9:17). We need to risk having nothing to say and nothing to pray. We need to learn to ask God and then wait for him to take the lead.

As soon as we move away from dependence on prayer lists and habits, we may begin to feel insecure. What are we going to do? What is going to happen? We need to resist the temptation to break our tension with a praise chorus or some other diversion.

Next, we may sense the Holy Spirit's leading and direction. Do we dare to share this in the group? What if we get it wrong? We might just sound silly. What will others think? Are we willing to take a risk?

What is our attitude when others share? Do we create an atmosphere of judgment and criticism, or one conducive to openness and acceptance? While we certainly need to 'test everything', we can do so together in an atmosphere of love and gentleness.

Test Everything

When we pray in the Spirit, the Holy Spirit leads us into new ways of praying. In a sense, we begin exploring 'uncharted territory'. Guidance from the Holy Spirit may seem largely intuitive and subjective. Any leading or impression could come from three possible sources: our own spirit, an evil spirit, or the Holy Spirit. How can we stay on course? How can we tell one voice from another?

Jesus himself assures us that we can tell his voice from other voices,

> *'The watchman opens the gate for him, and the sheep listen to his voice. He calls his own sheep by name and leads them out. When he has brought out all his own, he goes on ahead of them, and his sheep follow him because they know his voice. But they will never follow a stranger; in fact, they will run away from him because they do not recognize a stranger's voice.'*
>
> (John 10:3–5)

How do we recognize anyone's voice? By being familiar with it. We can easily recognize our close friend's voice on the telephone. Someone trying to impersonate our friend would not easily deceive us. An intimate, personal relationship with God is our best defense against deception.

God's voice always agrees with God's word. God does not contradict himself. He will not lead us contrary to his word. The person who fills himself with God's word has little trouble recognizing God's voice.

Obeying God's word helps assure us that we are not led astray. Jesus said, *'If anyone chooses to do God's will, he will find out whether my teaching comes from God or whether I speak on my own'* (John 7:17). When we walk in disobedience to God's clearly revealed will, we are easily deceived. People already involved in adulterous relationships may believe God is telling them to divorce their spouses, in spite of the fact that God's word clearly teaches against both adultery and divorce. Willful disobedience to God's clearly revealed word predisposes us to deception.

There is yet another way we can tell the source of any voice – the fruit test.

> *'Watch out for false prophets. They come to you in sheep's clothing, but inwardly they are ferocious wolves. By their fruit you will recognize them. Do people pick grapes from thorn bushes, or figs from thistles? Likewise every good tree bears good fruit, but a bad tree bears bad fruit. A good tree cannot bear bad fruit, and a bad tree cannot bear good fruit. Every tree that does not bear good fruit is cut down and thrown into the fire. Thus, by their fruit you will recognize them.'*
>
> (Matthew 7:15–20)

While this passage is speaking particularly about how to recognize false prophets, we can apply it to any type of voice or leading. This test may take time, but it is very reliable. Where has this voice been leading us? Does this voice seek only to glorify the Lord Jesus Christ? Are we growing in holy living and godly behavior? Are we being led into a deeper and more dynamic relationship with Jesus Christ? Are we growing in love for the Lord and others? Are the death and resurrection of Jesus Christ central features in our spiritual life? Are his purposes and ways becoming ours? Are we growing in discipleship and obedience? 'Yes' answers to such questions are signs of good fruit.

The final test for any leading or voice takes place in the assembly of believers. *'Two or three prophets should speak, and the others should weigh carefully what is said'* (1 Corinthians 14:29). Discernment belongs to the body of Christ. If I am hearing God's voice, others will be, too. We can expect that they will be hearing much the same thing. Each of us has only a tiny part of the picture, *'For we know in part and we prophesy in part . . . '* (1 Corinthians

13:9). Together we will be able to assemble the pieces and discern more clearly God's direction.

Making Room for the Holy Spirit

Paul wrote to the Corinthians about their meetings. *'What then shall we say, brothers? When you come together, everyone has a hymn, or a word of instruction, a revelation, a tongue or an interpretation. All these must be done for the strengthening of the church'* (1 Corinthians 14:26). This verse tells us two very important principles about meeting together. Firstly, *'everyone has.'* Everyone has something to contribute when we gather together. We must make room for one another, so that all can share. Small prayer groups provide an ideal setting for this. Secondly, the purpose of what we share is to strengthen the church.

Groups who want to experience more of the Holy Spirit's leading in prayer and intercession may find the following guidelines helpful. These points will be especially helpful for groups who want to break out of habitual patterns of prayer.[5]

1.   Everyone has something to contribute! That is wonderful. We need to conduct our meeting so that everyone has the opportunity to share. Leaders need to foster an encouraging, non-critical atmosphere and to actively encourage everyone to share.

2.   Listen to the Lord. Prayer is communication with God. Communication, by its very definition, is two-way. We talk to God and he talks to us. Before the meeting, we need to prepare our hearts by looking to the Lord, listening to him, and asking him to speak to us. During the meeting, we need to continue to listen.

3.   Groups may find a time of worship helpful in focusing their attention on the Lord. This should

105

not be a time of just singing songs, but of using music to draw close to the Lord together.

4. Group members may need to consciously lay down their own thoughts, requests and agendas and seek to submit to the Holy Spirit's leading of the group.

5. In order to avoid wasting time 'sharing needs' and thus losing valuable prayer time, I strongly suggest that there be no sharing time. The group can move directly into listening and prayer. Avoid the very awkward practice of telling the Lord the details of a situation when you actually intend to give the group information. This makes the group into eavesdroppers. God knows the details already, but he will not be offended if we interrupt our prayer to explain something to the group.

6. Do not be afraid of silences. Do not feel compelled to fill times of silence. Learn to wait before the Lord together.

7. Share what the Lord gives you. Perhaps the Lord will give you a song, a Scripture, a word or a prayer. Share what he gives you, but do not go on and on. Make room for one another.

8. Pray by subject as the Holy Spirit leads. Continue to pray about each subject until the group agree they are finished with it.

9. Pray short sentence-type prayers. Each individual's prayer does not need a formal opening and closing. The collective contributions of the group together often form one or a number of complete prayers.

10. Be sensitive. Listen to how the Holy Spirit is leading others. Listen to how the Holy Spirit is leading the group as a whole. Do not be surprised if one meeting is very different from another. Through the leading of the Holy Spirit, you will enter a new and exciting world of prayer and intercession.

Father, teach me to pray in the Spirit. Teach me to recognize what is of the flesh and what is of your Spirit. Lead me into the fellowship of intercession, as a member of the body of Christ. Make me sensitive, Lord, about keeping confidences. *'Set a guard over my mouth, O Lord; keep watch over the door of my lips. Let not my heart be drawn to what is evil...'* (Psalm 141:3–4). Show me any ways in which I grieve or quench your Spirit and give me a repentant heart. Set me free from prayer habits which hinder your Holy Spirit. Protect me from going astray. Help me to fix my eyes upon Jesus, the Author and Perfecter of our faith. May Jesus Christ fill my vision and may your glory be my goal. Amen.

Notes

1. *Webster's New World Dictionary of the American Language*, Second College Edition. World Publishing Co., 1980, p. 1251.
2. Song of Songs 4:12–5:1.
3. John 5:19–20, 30, 7:16–18, 8:15–16, 26, 28–29, 38, 42, 10:18, 27–30, 12:49–50, 14:31, 16:15, 17:4.
4. Matthew 14:23–25; Mark 1:35; Luke 5:16, 6:12, 9:18, 28–29, 11:1, 22:39–46.
5. Groups may like to experiment with different prayer styles. Here are a few suggestions:

    Prayer walking is simply walking while praying. This may be done individually or in groups. Different kinds of prayer walking have different purposes.

    Reconnaissance – to get a sense of the spiritual climate of an area. Informally, this may be best done individually or in two's and three's. This kind of investigation may be general or detailed, simple or complex. Resources: *Spiritual Mapping Field Guide*, by George Otis, Jr. Sentinel Group, PO Box 6334, Lynnwood, WA 98036. 1993. *Awakening Our Cities for God – Prayer Walking*, by Steve Hawthorne and Graham Kendrick. Milton Keynes, UK. Word Books. 1993.

Praise Marches – such as 'March for Jesus'. Involves public praise, prayer and proclamations. Resource: *March for Jesus*, by Kendrick, Coates, Forster, Green. Eastbourne, UK. Kingsway. 1992.

'Jericho' Marches – for breaking spiritual strongholds over specific areas (see Joshua 6:1–21).

Prayer walking to claim land (see Joshua 1:2–3).

One winter I became concerned about the park near our home. As I walked through it daily to buy groceries, I felt overwhelmed because of the large number of purposeless and lonely elderly people who spent their days there. So every time I walked through the park, I cried to God to save them. I did not know it at the time, but another missionary was praying similarly from her balcony which overlooked the park. That summer, the park became the focus of her evangelism training outreach and more than 200 people came to the Lord.

Groups may like to visit other groups who pray using different styles. For example, some groups pray:
- liturgical prayers, or prayers written out in advance
- all out loud at the same time – a common practice in China
- while walking around the room
- using lots of shouting, clapping, praise singing and proclamation.
- using the whole body in prayer: walking, clapping, kneeling, standing, and lying prostrate.

Chapter 4

God's Weapons

'... in truthful speech and in the power of God; with weapons of righteousness in the right hand and in the left...'   (2 Corinthians 6:7)

Offense or Defense?

Which will it be? Offense or defense? Are we to storm the gates of hell or should we battle only to maintain our position of safety in Christ Jesus?

'It is not wise to mess with the devil,' some advise. 'After all, he is bigger and more powerful than we are. He has millennia of experience and is very crafty. Maybe "spiritual giants" can take on the devil, but not ordinary Christians.' What about this advice? Can we ordinary Christians with all our weaknesses and struggles with besetting sins really triumph over Satan? Yes! While it may be true that Satan is more powerful and experienced than we are, it simply does not follow that he therefore wins.

First of all, his power is stolen power. He operates with usurped authority (Isaiah 14:13–15). He has already been judged and stands condemned (John 16:11, 12:31). All that remains is for his sentence to be executed (Revelation 20:10).

Secondly, we do not stand on our own against Satan. We are standing **in Christ Jesus**, the one who has already vanquished Satan. Satan would very much like us to believe we are no match for him. He may taunt, 'You can't do anything. Look how weak and foolish you are. You're a nobody, a nothing.' Do not listen to him. The battle is not won by the strong of this world. Listen instead to God: *'My grace is sufficient for you, for my power is made perfect in weakness'* (2 Corinthians 12:9). The Apostle Paul who penned those words knew that weakness is a prerequisite for receiving God's strength (2 Corinthians 12:10). He turned his back on this world's power because he understood that '... *God chose the foolish things of the world to shame the wise; God chose the weak things of the world to shame the strong'* (1 Corinthians 1:27). God's mighty warriors are his little sheep. It is God's weak ones who triumph.

Another favorite tactic of Satan is to remind us we are sinners, and just yesterday we did such-and-such. 'You might as well give up,' he says. 'No way will God answer **your** prayer. Just look how bad you are!' How can we handle such accusations? If Satan's accusations involve unconfessed sin, we should immediately confess it, ask for and receive God's forgiveness. If the accusation involves sin we have already confessed, we can simply inform the enemy (and remind ourselves) that this sin is already under the blood of Jesus. If such accusations persist, we can memorize scriptures which declare God's complete eradication of our sin. (For example: Psalm 103:3–12; Isaiah 43:25; Micah 7:18–19; Romans 8:1–2.) Many of us have been pushed into a corner by guilt and accusation. Here we sit, out of action, invisibly chained and silently suffering. It is time to break free. It is time to stop listening to Satan and to believe God's word. Our chains will drop off when struck with the sword of God's word.

Satan's accusations will collapse under the truth of God's word.

Thirdly, while Satan is experienced in sin, wickedness and every evil thing that produces death, he knows absolutely nothing of truth or light. He cannot understand the cross of Jesus Christ. Neither can he comprehend God's superior weapons such as love, forgiveness, blessing, mercy and praise. God gives us weapons and strategy against which Satan has no defense. If we try to battle Satan on his terms, using his weapons, we will certainly lose. But standing in Christ Jesus, using the weapons and strategy God provides, we will surely triumph.

Finally, both Jesus' actions and his words indicate that he himself went on the offense against Satan. We are his followers. When controversy arose over his expulsion of a demon, Jesus explained, *'When a strong man, fully armed, guards his own house, his possessions are safe. But when someone stronger attacks and overpowers him, he takes away the armor in which the man trusted and divides up the spoils'* (Luke 11:21-22). A significant part of Jesus' mission was to destroy the devil's work (1 John 3:8). When seventy-two of his disciples returned from preaching the gospel, healing the sick and casting out demons, Jesus told them, *'I saw Satan fall like lightning from heaven. I have given you authority to trample on snakes and scorpions and to overcome all the power of the enemy; nothing will harm you'* (Luke 10:18-19).

When I began to believe what God's word says about spiritual warfare and to act on it, it was not long before I experienced some counter-attacks from the enemy. The more fearful I became, the more I wavered. Maybe I had misunderstood God's word – maybe I was being presumptuous. Desperately I asked God, 'Do you **really** want us to take on Satan and attack his strongholds? He graciously answered me with a verse of scripture that put

111

all my doubts and fears to rest and enabled me to move ahead confidently in Christ Jesus: *'A wise man attacks the city of the mighty and pulls down the stronghold in which they trust'* (Proverbs 21:22).

> Heavenly Father, I thank you that I am in Christ Jesus, who has *'disarmed the powers and authorities'* and *'made a public spectacle of them, triumphing over them by the cross'* (Colossians 2:15). Help me not to be afraid in the face of my adversary who roars like a lion and who seeks to destroy me. I trust you to give me wisdom and strength to pull down Satan's strongholds and to experience your victory. I trust in you, my Shield and my Defender. *'... thanks be to God, who always leads us in triumphal procession in Christ, and through us spreads everywhere the fragrance of the knowledge of him'* (2 Corinthians 2:14). Amen.

The Nature of Our Weapons

> *'For though we live in the world, we do not wage war as the world does. The weapons we fight with are not the weapons of the world. On the contrary, they have divine power to demolish strongholds. We demolish arguments and every pretension that sets itself up against the knowledge of God, and we take captive every thought to make it obedient to Christ.'*
>
> (2 Corinthians 10:3–5)

Remember ex-prisoner Joe? His training included weaponry recognition and use. His new weapons were different from the weapons of his old captors. He did not even know what some of them were, let alone how to use them. Like Joe, we need weapons training.

We are all well acquainted with how the world wages

war. The array of weapons and their capacity for destruction staggers our minds – everything from antipersonnel mines which maim or kill their hapless victims to 'smart' hi-tech missiles which use TV and computer to lock on to their carefully chosen targets. From the simplest Molotov cocktail to the most sophisticated 'Star Wars' laser they are all, by nature, both violent and destructive.

The weapons of this world tear apart, damage, destroy and kill. Their effects reveal something of their source, just as surely as we can recognize a tree by its fruit (Matthew 7:20). Who kills? The devil. *'He was a murderer from the beginning... '* (John 8:44). Satan is also called *'the thief'* who *'comes only to steal and kill and destroy'* while Jesus came to give us life and give it abundantly (John 10:10).

The weapons of this world are incapable of building up and they are powerless to give life. Since these are the only weapons we have ever known, we inadvertently bring our worldly concept of weapons with us when we try to understand spiritual weapons. The weapons God gives us, however, are full of his life and power. They destroy only enemy strongholds like deception, pride, sin, bondage, and death. They release truth, humility, righteousness, freedom and life.

Not For Us – Judgment and Vengeance

Before we discuss the weapons God has given us, let us look at two weapons God reserves for himself. They are judgment and vengeance. A survey of scripture makes clear that judgment belongs to the Lord (Deuteronomy 1:17; 1 Corinthians 4:4–5; John 5:22, 27, 30). Those who judge do so by appointment and under the authorities instituted by God.[1] God commands that we not judge one another.

'Who are you to judge someone else's servant? To his own master he stands or falls. And he will stand, for the Lord is able to make him stand … You, then, why do you judge your brother? Or why do you look down on your brother? For we will all stand before God's judgment seat … Therefore, let us stop passing judgment on one another. Instead, make up your mind not to put any stumbling block or obstacle in your brother's way.' (Romans 14:4, 10, 13)

God has appointed a time for judgment.

'Therefore, judge nothing before the appointed time; wait till the Lord comes. He will bring to light what is hidden in darkness and will expose the motives of men's hearts. At that time each will receive his praise from God.' (1 Corinthians 4:5)

Jesus Christ is God's appointed judge. *'Moreover, the Father judges no one but has entrusted all judgment to the Son, that all may honor the Son just as they honor the Father … And he has given him authority to judge because he is the Son of Man'* (John 5:22, 27).

Jesus Christ is the only righteous judge and we are commanded to leave judgment to him. In prayer and intercession, our heart condition is crucial. If we harbor a spirit of judgment, we will end up giving place to a whole host of nasty stuff. Criticism, spite, contempt, scorn, fault-finding, slander, censure, disapproval, and rejection are all born out of a spirit of judgment. If we carry these around inside us, we will pray polluted prayers rather than Spirit-led ones. May we *'Speak and act as those who are going to be judged by the law that gives freedom, because judgment without mercy will be shown to anyone who has not been merciful. Mercy triumphs over judgment!'* (James 2:12–13). How dare we harbor judgment against those for whom we pray? May we cry 'mercy' for them as we do for ourselves.

The other weapon God reserves for himself is vengeance.

> *'The LORD looked and was displeased that there was no justice. He saw that there was no one, he was appalled that there was no one to intervene; so his own arm worked salvation for him, and his own righteousness sustained him. He put on righteousness as his breastplate, and the helmet of salvation on his head; he put on the garments of vengeance and wrapped himself in zeal as a cloak. According to what they have done, so will he repay wrath to his enemies and retribution to his foes; he will repay the islands their due.'* (Isaiah 59:15–18)

Most verses in the Bible appear only once. A number occur twice, but only a few have the special distinction of being repeated three times. One of these, Deuteronomy 32:35, *'It is mine to avenge; I will repay,'* is repeated in Hebrews 10:30 and Romans 12:19. The passage in Romans expands on the Old Testament teaching.

> *'Do not repay anyone evil for evil. Be careful to do what is right in the eyes of everybody. If it is possible, as far as it depends on you, live at peace with everyone. Do not take revenge, my friends, but leave room for God's wrath, for it is written: "It is mine to avenge; I will repay," says the Lord. On the contrary:*
>   *"If your enemy is hungry, feed him;*
>   *if he is thirsty, give him something to drink.*
>   *In doing this, you will heap burning coals on his*
>   *head."*
> *Do not be overcome by evil, but overcome evil with good.'* (Romans 12:17–21)

Jesus taught, *'Love your enemies, and pray for those who persecute you, that you may be sons of your Father in heaven'* (Matthew 5:44–45). We must not take our revenge in prayer. For us there can be no, 'Did you see what he did to me, God? Get him! Give him what he deserves!' God is gracious, and mercifully, he does not give us what we deserve. He wants us to behave like he behaves.

God's vengeance arises from his righteous judgments. But we desire vengeance to pay back those who hurt us. Our vengeance can be based only on our flawed, human perceptions and judgments, so there is no way we can execute righteous vengeance. The day for vengeance will come, and Jesus Christ himself will execute it (Revelation 19:11–21, 20:11–15). His judgments are righteous and true. May we learn to leave it to him.

> Lord Jesus, I confess that you are the righteous judge. You are perfect in mercy and judgment. Forgive me and cleanse me from harboring judgment in my heart. *'May the words of my mouth and the meditation of my heart be pleasing in your sight, O Lord, my Rock and my Redeemer'* (Psalm 19:14). *'Search me, O God, and know my heart; test me and know my anxious thoughts. See if there is any offensive way in me, and lead me in the way everlasting'* (Psalm 139:23–24).
>
> When my heart harbors judgment or the desire for vengeance, uncover it and help me to confess it. Cleanse me and lead me to trust you for righteous judgments and perfect vengeance. Help me to pray for everyone, especially my enemies, with love, mercy and blessing.

The Name of the Lord

God has given us a wide variety of weapons. Two of these are particularly important and deserve special attention:

> *'for you have exalted above all things*
>   *your name and your word.'*   (Psalm 138:2)

> *'Therefore God exalted him to the highest place and*
> *gave him the name that is above every name, that at*
> *the name of Jesus every knee should bow, in heaven*
> *and on earth and under the earth, and every tongue*
> *confess that Jesus Christ is Lord, to the glory of God*
> *the Father.'*   (Philippians 2:9–11)

Jesus is the name above all other names. His name
gives us protection (Proverbs 18:10), healing (Acts 3:6,
16), repentance and forgiveness (Luke 24:47), deliverance
(Acts 16:18), sonship (John 1:12) and life (John 20:31).

Jesus clearly instructed us to pray to God the Father in
Jesus' name (John 16:23–27). But what does it really mean
to pray in Jesus' name? *Webster's Dictionary* gives three
meanings for the phrase 'in the name of'.[2]

1.   as belonging to
2.   in appeal to
3.   in the authority of or as representative of

Each of these reflects an aspect of what it means to
pray in Jesus' name. We will consider each of these
individually in the context of David's confrontation with
Goliath.

1. As Belonging To

David was not a soldier and had no military training or
experience. Only a teenager and accustomed to looking
after sheep, he had been sent by his father to deliver
provisions to his brothers on the front lines. He arrived to
find the whole Israelite army immobilized by fear. Goliath,
the Philistine giant, had intimidated and threatened them
each morning and evening for forty days. When David
offered to fight Goliath, his words were soon carried to
King Saul's ears.

'David said to Saul, "Let no one lose heart on account of this Philistine; your servant will go and fight him."

Saul replied, "You are not able to go out against this Philistine and fight him; you are only a boy, and he has been a fighting man from his youth."

But David said to Saul, "Your servant has been keeping his father's sheep. When a lion or a bear came and carried off a sheep from the flock, I went after it, struck it and rescued the sheep from its mouth. When it turned on me, I seized it by its hair, struck it and killed it. Your servant has killed both the lion and the bear; this uncircumcised Philistine will be like one of them, because he has defied the armies of the living God. The LORD who delivered me from the paw of the lion and the paw of the bear will deliver me from the hand of this Philistine."

Saul said to David, "Go, and the LORD be with you."'   (1 Samuel 17:32–37)

David was so secure in his relationship with God that he not only offered to fight the Philistine, but he was also sure of victory. David knew he would triumph because he belonged to the Lord whom Goliath had defied.

2. In Appeal To

'Then Saul dressed David in his own tunic. He put a coat of armor on him and a bronze helmet on his head. David fastened on his sword over the tunic and tried walking around, because he was not used to them.

"I cannot go in these," he said to Saul, "because I am not used to them." So he took them off. Then he took his staff in his hand, chose five smooth stones from the stream, and put them in the pouch of his shepherd's bag and, with his sling in his hand, approached the Philistine.'   (1 Samuel 17:38–40)

David tried on Saul's clothing and armor, but discarded them for his familiar shepherd's garb because he was not used to them. It seemed crazy. How could he hope to defeat a gigantic, heavily-armed soldier without armor and weapons? But David was not trusting in armor and weapons. Neither was he trusting in his own strength and ability. David opposed this Philistine *'in the name of the Lord'*. His appeal was to God and to God alone. His rejection of Saul's armor and weapons provides an unmistakable and dramatic demonstration that he appealed to God alone for victory.

3. In the Authority Of, As Representative Of

'Meanwhile, the Philistine, with his shield bearer in front of him, kept coming closer to David. He looked David over and saw that he was only a boy, ruddy and handsome, and he despised him. He said to David, "Am I a dog, that you come at me with sticks?" And the Philistine cursed David by his gods. "Come here," he said, "and I'll give your flesh to the birds of the air and the beasts of the field!"

David said to the Philistine, "You come against me with the sword and spear and javelin, but I come against you in the name of the LORD Almighty, the God of the armies of Israel, whom you have defied. This day the LORD will hand you over to me, and I'll strike you down and cut off your head. Today I will give the carcasses of the Philistine army to the birds of the air and the beasts of the earth, and the whole world will know that there is a God in Israel. All those gathered here will know that it is not by sword or spear that the LORD saves; for the battle is the LORD's and he will give all of you into our hands."'

(1 Samuel 17:40–47)

How clear the battle line! How unmistakable the central issue. This was not a battle between a teenage shepherd boy from Judah and a huge blood-thirsty Philistine warrior, and David knew it. It was a battle between the Lord Almighty and those who defied him. This was not David the shepherd boy, blabbering presumptuous and foolish threats. This was David, who belonged to the Lord, speaking by God's authority. When David stood before Goliath and the armies of Israel and Philistia, he was speaking and acting *'in the name of the LORD'*.

We see the purpose in verse 47: *'All those gathered here will know that it is not by sword or spear that the LORD saves; for the battle is the LORD's, and he will give all of you into our hands.'*

It is the same for us today:

1.   God does not save by man's strength.
2.   We do not wage war as the world does.
3.   The battle belongs to the Lord.
4.   His victory has already been secured.
5.   God receives the glory.

Four times Jesus tells the disciples to make their requests to the Father in Jesus' name: (John 14:12–14, 15:7, 12–17, 16:23–27). In these verses God promises us that we will do greater things than Jesus did (John 14:12), that he will do whatever we ask (John 14:14, 15:16, 16:23), and that our joy will be complete (John 16:24). What amazing promises there are for those who ask in Jesus' name. But these promises are conditional. We must love one another (John 15:12, 17). We must remain in Jesus, and his words must remain in us (John 15:7).

As his representatives on earth, Jesus wants us to show forth his character, speak his words, do his works, and **pray his will.**

4. Not a Magic Word

'You shall not misuse the name of the LORD your God, for the LORD will not hold anyone guiltless who misuses his name.' (Exodus 20:7)

When we think of misusing the Lord's name, most of us think of cursing or using God's name as a joke. But these are not the only ways of misusing God's name. What about expecting God to answer our prayer because we speak the right words, the right formula? What about using God's name as a magic word? What is in our hearts when we pray 'in Jesus' name' at the end of our prayers? Somewhere in our minds do we think that by adding this phrase – by saying the magic words – our prayer will be answered? Do we believe God answers because we utter the right incantation? What is in our hearts?

The prophet Malachi was concerned about the hearts of God's servants in his day.

' "For I am a great king," says the LORD Almighty, "and my name is to be feared among the nations. And now this admonition is for you, O priests. If you do not listen, and if you do not set your heart to honor my name," says the LORD Almighty, "I will send a curse upon you, and I will curse your blessings. Yes, I have already cursed them, because you have not set your heart to honor me." ' (Malachi 1:14b–2:2)

While Malachi's words were addressed to Israel's priests, they apply to us today as well, because we also are *'a chosen people, a royal priesthood, a holy nation, a people belonging to God...'* (1 Peter 2:9). God brought three charges against Israel's priests. They did not fear the name of the Lord, they did not listen, and they did not set their hearts to honor the Lord's name.

If God's people, his own children, do not fear his name,

how will the nations learn to do so? If we refuse to listen to God and to honor his name, he will make our prayers of blessing into curses. How important it is for us to fear and honor God's name. God will not bless the misuse of his name.

> *'What causes fights and quarrels among you? Don't they come from your desires that battle within you? You want something but don't get it. You kill and covet, but you cannot have what you want. You quarrel and fight. You do not have, because you do not ask God. When you ask, you do not receive, because you ask with wrong motives, that you may spend what you get on your pleasures.'* (James 4:1–3)

God is interested in our motivation. Is our goal our own worldly pleasures? Is it because we want what we want when we want it? We cannot just plug in the words 'in Jesus' name' at the end of our prayers and get what we want. We cannot expect God to honor our prayers with his blessings and answers when our hearts are not set to honor his name. Praying in Jesus' name means that we honor his name by obeying his commands, that we make God's desires and will our own, and that we pray in union with Christ Jesus himself.

> Lord Jesus, thank you for giving us the command and privilege of praying in your name. Forgive me for the times I have misused your name or reduced your name to a magic word. Please forgive me for the times when I have not feared your name or listened to you, and when I have not set my heart to honor your name. Please increase my understanding and experience of praying in Jesus' name. Lord, I belong to you. Help me to appeal only to you and to pray with your authority. Make me desire what you

desire, and teach me how to pray according to your will. Amen.

The Sword of the Spirit – the Word of God

'This is the one I esteem: he who is humble and contrite in spirit, and trembles at my word.'   (Isaiah 66:2b)

Just for a moment, imagine yourself in battle alongside our friend Joe. There you are, clad in the armor of God. Suddenly the enemy is upon you – not miles or even yards away, but right in your face. You draw your sword and lift it high. To your surprise and horror it is hopelessly short. It looks dull and unpolished, but worst of all, it is drooping limply to one side like a flabby piece of rubber. The enemy slowly smiles, icy and cruel, while cold fear rushes up your back and threatens to overwhelm you.

Fantasy? Yes, but it illustrates an all too common experience. Many of us are standing on the spiritual battlefield with stubby, dull, or flabby swords. What has gone wrong? The problem is that we do not know God's word. Some of us have stubby swords. We know portions of God's word. Maybe we know the New Testament quite well, but we are unacquainted with the Old Testament. Some of us have dull swords. We once knew God's word fairly well, but neglect of daily Bible reading and prayer has caused us to lose our edge. Some of us have flabby swords. We read God's word and we try to apply it, but it seems little more than stories of long ago and far away. We find it boring and irrelevant, and it rarely causes us to tremble.

If we are to experience the triumph of Jesus Christ on the spiritual battlefield, our sword, the word of God, must be sharp, clean and well cared for. And we must know how to use it in battle against the enemy.

When we talk about the word of God, just what do we mean? Certainly we mean the Bible, but there is more. God's word is a wonderful subject for extensive study. God's word:

- is eternal (Psalm 119:89; Isaiah 40:8; Matthew 24:35)
- nourishes (Deuteronomy 8:3; Matthew 4:4; Psalm 119:103; Psalm 19:10)
- is perfect (Psalm 19:7; Psalm 119:96)
- gives light (Psalm 119:105, 130; 2 Peter 1:19)
- is precious (Psalm 19:10; Psalm 119:72, 162)
- makes wise (Psalm 119:98–100)
- is seed (Mark 4:3, 14; 1 Peter 1:23)
- is guaranteed fruitful (Isaiah 55:10–11)
- is alive (1 Peter 1:23; Hebrews 4:12–13)
- gives new birth (1 Peter 1:23)

And this just scratches the surface. God's word is full of mystery. What exactly is the word of God? God's word includes his written word (the Bible),[3] his spoken word,[4] and God's word made flesh – Jesus Christ.[5] We cannot understand these with human reasoning and wisdom – we need spiritual understanding from God himself.

While these three things that we call the word of God seem separate and distinct, at the same time, we cannot really separate them from one another. For example, we know from Genesis 1 that God created the heavens and the earth by his spoken word. Hebrews 1:1–3 tells us, *'In the past God spoke to our forefathers through the prophets at many times and in various ways, but in these last days he has spoken to us by his Son, whom he appointed heir of all things, and through whom he made the universe. The Son is the radiance of God's glory and the exact representation of his being, sustaining all things by his powerful word.'* This identifies Jesus Christ as our creator and sustainer – God's spoken word (see also Psalm 33:6–9 and Colossians 1:14–17).

Matthew 5:17–18 and John 5:39–40 reveal that Jesus is the fulfillment of God's written word. Revelation 14:13 shows God's spoken word becoming his written word as God commanded John to write it down. God's written word, spoken word and Word made flesh are interrelated and inseparable.

> *'In the beginning was the Word, and the Word was with God, and the Word was God. He was with God in the beginning. Through him all things were made; without him nothing was made that has been made ... The Word became flesh and made his dwelling among us. We have seen his glory, the glory of the One and Only, who came from the Father, full of grace and truth.'*   (John 1:1–3, 14)

> *'I saw heaven standing open and there before me was a white horse, whose rider is called Faithful and True. With justice he judges and makes war. His eyes are like blazing fire, and on his head are many crowns. He has a name written on him that no one knows but he himself. He is dressed in a robe dipped in blood, and his name is the Word of God. The armies of heaven were following him, riding on white horses and dressed in fine linen, white and clean. Out of his mouth comes a sharp sword with which to strike down the nations. "He will rule them with an iron scepter." He treads the winepress of the fury of the wrath of God Almighty. On his robe and on his thigh he has this name written:*
> *KING OF KINGS AND LORD OF LORDS.'*
>   (Revelation 19:11–16)

The Word of God – we need a picture of just who this is. This is Jesus Christ, the living and enduring Word of God. Then we will tremble at God's word and come humbly before him to receive instruction. Before long, we will find that our swords have become long, sharp, and strong.

'Sure, I believe in Jesus,' Jenny told me. 'But I really can't get into the Bible. Every time I read it, it makes me uncomfortable. So I don't read it much.' Actually, Jenny tried hard to avoid reading the Bible at all. She did not even like to hold it during group Bible studies. Jenny wanted Jesus, but she did not want the Bible. She wanted to have a relationship with Jesus, but she did not want to obey God's word. Not surprisingly, her spiritual growth was painfully slow and devoid of joy and peace.

Jenny is not alone. Many Christians try to accept Jesus while they reject his word. Those who continue in this path of such profound contradiction cannot grow in Christ. We need both a personal relationship with Jesus and obedience to God's word. *'Those who obey his commands live in him, and he in them'* (1 John 3:24). We cannot accept Jesus and reject his word.

Do Not Shrink from God's Word

God's word is uncomfortable. It pricks our consciences, convicts us of sin, judges our hearts, and gives us a sentence of death. No wonder we feel like avoiding it. The Apostle Paul experienced this: *'I found that the very commandment that was intended to bring life actually brought death'* (Romans 7:10). Yes, God's word will put us to death. But this is what it is supposed to do.

Jesus Christ said that he is the resurrection and the life (John 11:25). But resurrection life is available only to dead people. We must submit to God's word, allow it to convict us of sin, and let it put us to death. We must follow Jesus to the cross so we can receive his resurrection life. May we not shrink away from God's word when we feel it begin to put us to death. But may we press on obediently through death so we can experience the fullness of Jesus' resurrection life.

If we are to 'take ... *the sword of Spirit, which is the word of God*' (Ephesians 6:17), and wield this powerful weapon against the enemy, we must recognize whose sword this is. This is the sword of the Holy Spirit, and it is he who uses it.

> 'For the word of God is living and active. Sharper than any double-edged sword, it penetrates even to dividing soul and spirit, joints and marrow; it judges the thoughts and attitudes of the heart. Nothing in all creation is hidden from God's sight. Everything is uncovered and laid bare before the eyes of him to whom we must give account.'　　　(Hebrews 4:12-13)

This is a double-edged sword. The Holy Spirit uses it both through us and on us. Like a knife in the hands of a skilled surgeon, the sword of the Spirit cuts and hurts, but it brings us healing and life.

> '...a two-edged sword
> Of heavenly temper keen
> And double were the wounds it made
> Where it glanced between.
> 'Twas death to sin; 'twas life
> To all who mourned for sin.
> It kindled and it silenced strife,
> Made war and peace within.'　　(E.M. Bounds)[6]

I believe that the Holy Spirit is able to use his sword through us to the same extent that we allow him to use it on us. Jesus has been given all authority and power because of his perfect obedience. Jesus had such respect for the written word of God that he yielded himself obediently to it in every detail. He told his disciples, 'Everything must be fulfilled that is written about me in the Law of Moses, the Prophets and the Psalms' (Luke 24:44), and '... the world must learn that I love the Father and *that I do exactly what my Father has commanded me'* (John 14:31). No wonder Jesus spoke God's word with authority, overcoming Satan with it. Three times Satan tempted him and three times Jesus answered him beginning with the phrase, *'It is written . . . '* (Matthew 4:4, 7, 10).

When I was a little girl and playmates made fun of me, my mother taught me a rhyme with which to answer them, 'Sticks and stones can break my bones, but names can never hurt me.' While my mother intended to equip me to withstand life's hard knocks, she was mistaken about the power of our words. The less sophisticated neighborhood taunt, 'I'm rubber, you're glue, and everything you say bounces off me and sticks back to you,' was more popular than my mother's rhyme, no doubt because it acknowledged the truth that words can hurt and even incorporated a curse as a defense.

God's word says, *'The tongue has the power of life and death'* (Proverbs 18:21), and *'Reckless words pierce like a sword, but the tongue of the wise brings healing'* (Proverbs 12:18). Small wonder, then, that under the direction of God's Spirit, our tongues can put Satan to flight. These are the words that drive out demons, bring freedom to captives, heal the sick, and comfort those who mourn.

God's word destroys his enemies. Addressing the church in Pergamum and warning those who teach wicked things, Jesus said, *'These are the words of him who has the sharp, double-edged sword . . . Repent therefore! Otherwise, I will soon come to you and will fight against them with the sword of my mouth'* (Revelation 2:12, 16). In 2 Thessalonians 2:8 we read about what will happen to God's enemies, *'And then the lawless one will be revealed, whom the Lord Jesus will overthrow with the breath of his mouth and destroy by the splendor of his coming.'* In Revelation 19:15 we see Jesus, the Word of God, riding at the head of the armies of heaven. *'Out of his mouth comes a sharp sword* with which to strike down the nations.' Jesus also said, 'There is a judge for the one who rejects me and does not accept my words; that very word which I spoke will condemn him at the last day' (John 12:48).

God's word creates and makes alive. It is by God's imperishable word that we are born again (1 Peter 1:23). In Romans we see how God gives us salvation by hearing, believing, and confessing his word.

> ' "The word is near you; it is in your mouth and in your heart," that is, the word of faith we are proclaiming. That if you confess with your mouth, "Jesus is Lord," and believe in your heart that God raised him from the dead, you will be saved. For it is with your heart that you believe and are justified, and it is with your mouth that you confess and are saved.'
>
> (Romans 10:8–10)

Jesus demonstrated the power of his word in the resurrection of Lazarus in John 11:38–44. His three-word command, 'Lazarus, come out!' was sufficient to resurrect a man who had lain dead in a tomb for four days. He was so full of life that he came out hopping, restrained only by his grave clothes.

One of the most striking examples of God's word in the mouth of a believer to make alive is found in Ezekiel 37. God commanded Ezekiel to prophesy to dry bones scattered across a valley. As he did, God's word caused them to come together with flesh and skin so they stood up a great army and received the breath of life.

Among all his earthly creatures, God has granted human beings the power and authority to speak his words. May God grant us grace to bring our tongues under his control so we may speak forth God's life-giving word.

God's word is established, sure, imperishable, and certain to be fulfilled, and this is the mighty weapon he invites us to take up. As we yield to God's word in obedience, the Holy Spirit will use his sword through us with power and authority. The enemy cannot stand before it. Those we pray for will receive healing and life.

> Almighty Father, make me humble and contrite, one who trembles at your word. In your mercy, give me a glimpse of Jesus Christ, the Word of God. Cause me to hunger and thirst for your word. *'Open my eyes that I may see wonderful things in your law. I am a stranger on earth; do not hide your commands from me. My soul is consumed with longing for your laws at all times'* (Psalm 119:18–20). May your word penetrate my heart, judging my thoughts and attitudes. May your word put my flesh to death and make my spirit alive. I invite you, Holy Spirit, to use your sword – your word – both on me and through me, to the glory of Jesus Christ. Amen.

Proclamation

> *'His intent was that now, through the church, the manifold wisdom of God should be made known to the rulers and authorities in the heavenly realms, according to his eternal purpose which he accomplished in Christ Jesus our Lord.'* (Ephesians 3:10)

> *'The Lord announced the word,*
> *and great was the company of those who*
> *proclaimed it.'* (Psalm 68:11)

'To proclaim' primarily means 'to announce publicly'. According to the *Collins English Dictionary*, it may also mean 'to show or indicate plainly' and 'to praise or extol'. The English word 'proclaim' comes from a Latin root meaning 'to shout aloud'.[7]

As a prayer weapon, we might define proclamation as an authoritative announcement spoken openly before heaven and earth. Our authority to make such public announcements rests with Jesus Christ, and our proclamations are in his name. To whom do we speak these proclamations? Some are spoken primarily for the benefit of people on earth, while others are for the ears of those in the heavenly realms.

Proclamations are primarily spoken, but at least one very important proclamation involves actions as well as words. In his instructions concerning the Lord's supper, Paul declares, *'for whenever you eat this bread and drink this cup, you proclaim the Lord's death until he comes'* (1 Corinthians 11:26). The action of celebrating the Lord's supper – of eating the bread and drinking the wine – proclaims the death and resurrection of Jesus Christ; it proclaims the gospel.

The most fundamental proclamation in the New Testament is the gospel.[8] After all, this is the Christian's message. The foundation of all other proclamations is the death and resurrection of Jesus Christ. What is the content of our proclamations? God's word, the gospel and the mighty things God has done.

In warfare prayer, proclamations may be declarations of Jesus' victory over Satan. The audience need not necessarily be an earthly one. In Christ Jesus, we have access into the heavenly realms through prayer. It is quite possible to stand alone in one's room and proclaim Christ's victory in the hearing of all the principalities and powers of heaven.

Satan hates prayer proclamations. Bold announcements of the truth frighten, confuse and anger him. He does not like to have his nose rubbed in the truth of Christ's victory and his own defeat. He hates to be reminded that when Jesus went to the cross, he *'disarmed the powers and authorities* [and] *made a public spectacle of them, triumphing over them by the cross'* (Colossians 2:15). Proclamations of the victory of Jesus Christ on the cross make the defeat of Satan a public spectacle all over again, while we give thanks to God, *'who always leads us in triumphal procession in Christ'* (2 Corinthians 2:14).

We do not have to invent proclamations. God's word is full of victorious truth we can proclaim. Proclamations can be sung or spoken. Our proclamations can span the past, present, and future. Some proclamations, like portions of God's word, will be prophetic in nature. The authoritative use of God's word in faith by proclamation can force Satan to give up territory he has usurped and set captives free. Scriptural proclamations are a way of wielding the God's word as a sword against the enemy. Combined with the authority of Jesus' name and faith, scripture proclamations are powerful weapons. Below are some scriptures that can be used as proclamations. You will be able to find many more.

1 Chronicles 16:23–36	Psalm 47
Psalm 89	Psalm 93
Psalm 110	Isaiah 9:6–7
Isaiah 45:21–25	Isaiah 52–53
Isaiah 62	Matthew 28:18
Philippians 2:6–11	Colossians 1:13–20
Hebrews 1:3–13	Revelation 5:6–14
Revelation 11:15	Revelation 15:3–4
Revelation 19:6–8	

The many names and titles in scripture for God the Father, Jesus Christ, and the Holy Spirit make excellent raw material for proclamation, as do many old hymns. Proclamations can also tell the mighty things God has done. We can proclaim what God has done in the Bible or in our own day. Moses' and Miriam's songs in Exodus 15 are good examples, and so is Peter's sermon in Acts 2:22–36.

Here is a somewhat lengthy proclamation about wickedness and corruption. (We are commanded to pray for all in authority, so let us remember to ask for God's light and truth for all who rule over us (1 Timothy 2:1–4).)

Righteousness and justice are the foundations of your throne, O Lord. Every throne and authority established in corruption will be cast down from its rotten foundations. *'Your throne, O God, will last for ever and ever; a scepter of justice will be the scepter of your kingdom. You love righteousness and hate wickedness; therefore God, your God has set you above your companions by anointing you with the oil of joy'* (Psalm 45:6–7 and Hebrews 1:8–9).

You, Lord Jesus Christ, are the Anointed One. It is your throne that lasts forever. Because you were obedient unto death, even death on a cross, God has exalted you to the highest place – with angels, authorities, and powers in submission to you. All authority in heaven and on earth belong to you. Though the nations rage and the peoples plot against you, though the kings of the earth take their stand and the rulers gather together against the Lord and his Anointed One, they cannot stand.

In Jesus' name, we declare that no corrupt throne or authority shall stand. Every one will be brought down in Jesus' name, and the Lord alone will be exalted in that day.[9]

Praise

'For the LORD takes delight in his people;
he crowns the humble with salvation.
Let the saints rejoice in this honor
and sing for joy on their beds.

> *May the praise of God be in their mouths*
> *and a double-edged sword in their hands.'*
>
> (Psalm 149:4–6)

God's weapons are full of his goodness, love and blessing. They are overwhelmingly positive. Satan uses criticism and accusation to tear down and destroy, while God builds up and encourages with praise.

Praise is powerful. This is memorably recorded in 2 Chronicles 20:1–30. An enormous army from Moab, Ammon and Seir was advancing upon the nation of Judah. Jehosaphat, the king, was alarmed and called the nation together to fast and seek God. Jehosaphat prayed publicly, acknowledging God's omnipotence, recalling his covenantal promises, and appealing to him for help. *'We do not know what to do,'* he prayed, *'but our eyes are upon you'* (2 Chronicles 20:12). And all the people – men, women, and children – stood before the Lord.

God answered with a prophetic word, giving them reassurance and comfort and telling them, *'the battle is not yours, but God's'* (2 Chronicles 20:15), and, *'You will not have to fight this battle. Take up your positions; stand firm and see the deliverance the LORD will give you, O Judah and Jerusalem. Do not be afraid; do not be discouraged. Go out to face them tomorrow, and the LORD will be with you'* (2 Chronicles 20:17). The people worshiped and praised God.

The next morning Jehosaphat assembled his army and exhorted them to have faith in God. Then, in what could only be called an absurd military strategy, he appointed singers to praise God and placed them at the head of his battle force. As they praised God, *'Give thanks to the LORD, for his love endures forever'* (2 Chronicles 20:21), God set ambushes among the enemy invaders and they destroyed one another. Jehosaphat's army found only dead bodies. It took them three days to carry away the plunder. They spent the fourth day praising God. The fear of the Lord fell upon the surrounding nations, giving Jehosaphat's kingdom peace.

National, corporate praise of the Lord resulted in an enduring victory which gave rest to an entire nation. How easily the weaponless singers at the head of Jehosaphat's army could have given way to fear or complained about being used as human shields. They chose to trust God for deliverance and to praise him as they walked forward towards the enemy and to what looked like certain death. The nation of Judah combined the powerful weapon of praise with faith and obedience to God's word. Using spiritual weapons, they triumphed over cold steel and real flesh and blood enemies. Earthly weapons of war may have become more powerful and deadly over the centuries, but God's spiritual weapons remain superior.

In prayer and intercession, praise is a wonderful weapon. Sometimes during prayer we can feel bogged down, overwhelmed by a sense of Satan's strength and the extent of his schemes. God may seem far away while evil seems deadly and near. Prayer becomes difficult because our focus has subtly shifted from the Lord to the problem and the enemy. Like Jehosaphat, we can easily become overwhelmed, alarmed and discouraged. At these times, it is helpful to simply stand and praise the Lord with psalms, hymns and spiritual songs.

In my experience, at some point during such times of praise, battling praise may give way to a sense of triumph, rejoicing and celebration. We experience a taste of God's victory. And since we know that God desires his will to be done on earth as it is in heaven (Matthew 6:10), I also expect some change or progress to be reflected in the earthly situation we are praying about.

Praising the Lord drives away fear and discouragement.

Jesus Christ, has given us *'a garment of praise instead of a spirit of despair'* (Isaiah 61:3). He has anointed us with his life-giving Spirit and given us the power of praise. When we, like Jehosaphat, find ourselves under attack and in desperate circumstances, let us lift up our eyes and voices to God. As we fix our eyes on Jesus, may we lift our hearts and voices to praise and thank him, for his love endures forever.

Praise is wonderfully practical. It brings blessing, encouragement and up-building. It is something we can exercise daily in all our relationships. Criticism is nothing but the poison of accusation with a slightly different flavor. Tearing down other people is easy, but we are called to build one another up.

It is no secret that children who receive much criticism and little praise often become discouraged and demotivated. When Hong Kong's annual exam results are released, school children commit suicide by jumping off skyscrapers in alarming numbers. Though reasons for this tragedy are complex, without question, criticism plays a large role. Parents, out of superstition or hoping to prevent their children from becoming conceited, often withhold all forms of praise while criticizing liberally. From the time they are born, many Hong Kong children receive a steady diet of, 'You are useless,' 'I don't want you,' 'You are so much trouble,' and 'Drop dead.' Many teachers perpetuate the abuse. In a distorted attempt to motivate they dish up deadly despair, 'You are stupid,' 'You are so lazy, you'll never succeed,' and 'You are no use.' In front of their classmates, teachers frequently ridicule and humiliate students who get poor marks. I cannot help but wonder how many could be rescued simply with words of encouragement and praise.

'Father, forgive me for the times I have given way to discouragement and despair. Forgive me for the times

136

I have torn down others with criticism. Fill me with
your Holy Spirit and teach me to use the weapon of
praise to bring down the enemy strongholds of
despair. Show me how to use praise to build up
and encourage everyone around me, especially my
family. Amen.'

Notes

1. Exodus 18:21–22; Deuteronomy 1:16–17, 25:1; 1 Corinthians
   5:12–13, 6:2–6; Romans 13:2.
2. *Webster's New World Dictionary of the American Language*,
   Second College Edition. World Publishing Co., 1980, p. 944.
3. 2 Timothy 3:16; 2 Peter 1:19–21; Romans 15:4.
4. Genesis 1:3; Psalm 33:6–9; Psalm 148:1–6.
5. John 1:1–3, 14; Revelation 19:11–16.
6. *Power Through Prayer*, by E.M. Bounds. Whitaker House,
   Springdale, PA, 1982, p. 79.
7. *The Collins English Dictionary*. William Collins Sons & Co., Ltd,
   Glasgow, 1979, 1986, p. 1220.
8. Acts 20:20–21 & 27; Romans 10:8–13, 15:14–17; 1 Corinthians
   11:26; Colossians 1:23, 28, 4:3.
9. Psalm 94:20, 37:20, 45:6, 97:2; Philippians 2:8–11; 1 Peter
   3:22; Matthew 28:18; Psalm 2:1–2; Acts 4:25–26 and Isaiah
   2:11.

Chapter 5

More Weapons

Forgiveness

> 'If you forgive anyone his sins, they are forgiven; if you
> do not forgive them, they are not forgiven.'
>
> (John 20:23)

Take a moment and read that verse again. Consider the
great power of the weapon Jesus has placed in our hands.
God has given us power to forgive.

'How can this be?' some may ask. 'Surely only God
forgives sins!' (Mark 2:7). 'Maybe a priest or minister can
forgive sins, but not every believer, not me. And how can
the forgiveness I may grant be like God's forgiveness?
Surely it cannot carry the same weight.'

What does Scripture say? All humans need forgiveness
because we are all sinners. Our sins separate us from God
(Isaiah 59:2). God the Father has given his Son, Jesus
Christ, authority to forgive sins. When Jesus healed a
paralyzed man at Capernaum, he told him, *'Son, your sins
are forgiven,'* rather than *'get up, take your mat and walk'*
in order *'that you may know that the Son of Man has
authority on earth to forgive sins.'* Jesus' authority was
demonstrated as the healed and forgiven man got up and
walked out (Mark 2:3, 9–10).

After his resurrection, when Jesus commissioned his followers to go and make disciples of all nations, he declared, *'All authority in heaven and on earth has been given to me'* (Matthew 28:18). God has given every believer real power to forgive sins and he is accepting no excuses for our not exercising it. He does not ask us determine blame or to demand that the other party meet our terms. In every situation, God requires that we forgive.

In words and actions, Jesus taught us to forgive in every circumstance. But we can become so familiar with Jesus' words that they lose their impact. A good example is the Lord's prayer. How many times have we prayed, *'Forgive us our debts as we have also forgiven our debtors'* (Matthew 6:12), without considering our words? We are asking God to forgive us to the same extent that we forgive others! When Jesus taught this prayer, he went on to emphasize: *'If you forgive men when they sin against you, your heavenly Father will also forgive you. But if you do not forgive men their sins, your Father will not forgive your sins'* (Matthew 6:14–15). Do we ever pause long enough to consider what this really means?

Luke's rendition of this prayer takes a positive approach, *'Forgive us our sins, for we also forgive everyone who sins against us'* (Luke 11:4). Well, do we? Is there anyone we have vowed not to forgive or perhaps just neglected to forgive? This binds both parties in unforgiveness.

Some of us are in the habit of excusing rather than forgiving one another. We meditate until we come up with enough excuses and extenuating circumstances to say we 'understand why he (or she or they) did it.' So we excuse the other person. But, dear ones, this is **not** forgiveness.

When we forgive, we do so in Christ Jesus. We acknowledge not only the offense against us, but also that we likewise are guilty offenders, forgiven only through the sacrifice of Jesus Christ. As partakers of his forgiveness, we must extend the same forgiveness to everyone who wounds or offends us. Failing to do so, we bind ourselves and others in unforgiveness.

May we not justify our unforgiveness with the words of Luke 17:3–4, *'If your brother sins, rebuke him, and if he repents, forgive him. If he sins against you seven times in a day, and seven times comes back to you and says, "I repent," forgive him.'* May we not say, 'I'm waiting for him to repent and admit he's wrong. I know I am in the right, so I'm not going to forgive him.' Jesus was not placing a limitation on forgiveness with these words. Rather, he was emphasizing that the forgiveness we extend should have no limits.

In another gospel, Jesus used a parable to illustrate that his forgiveness is complete and free.

> *Then Peter came to Jesus and asked, "Lord, how many times shall I forgive my brother when he sins against me? Up to seven times?"*
>
> *Jesus answered, "I tell you, not seven times, but seventy-seven times.*
>
> *"Therefore, the kingdom of heaven is like a king who wanted to settle accounts with his servants. As he began the settlement, a man who owed him ten thousand talents was brought to him. Since he was not able to pay, the master ordered that he and his wife and his children and all that he had be sold to repay the debt.*
>
> *"The servant fell on his knees before him. 'Be patient with me,' he begged, 'and I will pay back everything.' The servant's master took pity on him, canceled the debt and let him go.*
>
> *"But when that servant went out, he found one of his fellow servants who owed him a hundred denarii. He grabbed him and began to choke him. 'Pay back what you owe me!' he demanded.*

*"His fellow servant fell to his knees and begged him.
'Be patient with me, and I will pay you back.'*

*"But he refused. Instead he went off and had the
man thrown into prison until he could pay the debt.
When the other servants saw what had happened, they
were greatly distressed and went and told their master
everything that had happened.*

*"Then the master called the servant in. 'You wicked
servant,' he said, 'I canceled all that debt of yours
because you begged me to. Shouldn't you have had
mercy on your fellow servant just as I had on you?' In
anger his master turned him over to the jailers, until
he should pay back all he owed.*

*"This is how my heavenly Father will treat each of
you unless you forgive your brother from your heart."'*
(Matthew 18:21-36)

God has completely forgiven all our sins. He has not
waited until we are a little more sorry or until we can
guarantee we will not do it again. The main point of the
parable is clear. While God's forgiveness is free, undeserved and complete, it is also conditional. If we refuse to
extend to others the same forgiveness we have received
from God, we will find ourselves in the torment of
unforgiveness, bound by debts we can never repay.
Forgiving others is not optional. God forgives us the way
we forgive others. In this we should certainly fear God.
May we become extravagant forgivers.

It is possible to harbor unforgiveness on behalf of
someone else. During a time when my husband and I
could not agree which church to attend, I sought some
help. The roots of the difficulty were uncovered in minutes
when my counselors asked me about my former pastors.
Among these godly and wonderful men were four who had
fallen victim to marital unfaithfulness. I had no idea that

my current difficulties stemmed from unhealed wounds and my failure to forgive these men for hurting their wives, families, and churches – and yes, me.

In prayer, I forgave each one individually and specifically. My release was instantaneous and lasting. I was now free to relate properly to my husband and other male spiritual leaders. I also gained a new insight and sensitivity in how to pray for pastors and Christian leaders.

If there remain instances where we feel justified in withholding forgiveness, let us consider Jesus. As men cruelly executed him for crimes he did not commit, he covered them with forgiveness, *'Father, forgive them, for they do not know what they are doing'* (Luke 23:34). They did not repent, they were not sorry, and they did not ask for his forgiveness. Nevertheless, he freely gave it.

I believe we have authority and power to wield God's weapons in spiritual warfare to the extent that we allow the Holy Spirit to operate them in our own lives. If we are to effectively exercise forgiveness as a spiritual weapon, we ourselves need to become generous and practiced forgivers. Let us ask God to show us every area and instance where we can exercise the amazing weapon of forgiveness.

> Father, forgive me as I forgive everyone who sins against me. If I hold anyone in unforgiveness, please bring it to my attention and enable me to forgive completely and freely. Lord, teach me to use forgiveness as a spiritual weapon to set captives free and promote healing in the body of Christ and in society.

Mercy

> *'Mercy triumphs over judgment!'* (James 2:13)

God has given us a weapon that overcomes judgment. It is none other than misunderstood mercy. This world associates mercy with limp-willed, mushy indulgence. The world has no idea it is a powerful spiritual weapon.

The Oxford dictionary defines 'mercy' as, 'compassionate treatment of or attitude towards an offender, adversary, etc. who is in one's power or care'.[1] A synonym is 'grace',[2] which is often defined as 'undeserved favor'. Mercy and grace characterize God's treatment of us.

> *'But when the kindness and love of God our Savior appeared, he saved us, not because of righteous things we had done, but because of his mercy. He saved us through the washing of rebirth and renewal by the Holy Spirit, whom he poured out on us generously through Jesus Christ our Savior, so that, being justified by his grace, we might become heirs having the hope of eternal life.'* (Titus 3:4–7)

Not only are we recipients of God's mercy, but we are also to be generous givers. What we receive, we must freely give – especially to those who do not deserve it.

> *'But love your enemies, do good to them, and lend to them without expecting to get anything back. Then your reward will be great, and you will be sons of the Most High, because he is kind to the ungrateful and wicked. Be merciful, just as your Father is merciful.*
> *Do not judge, and you will not be judged. Do not condemn and you will not be condemned. Forgive and you will be forgiven.'* (Luke 6:35–37)

In order not to be judged, we must get rid of the judgments we hold against others. Judgment is terribly binding, and it is my guess that judgment imprisons as many people as does unforgiveness.

How do we form judgments? It is not difficult. Take Evelyn, for example. She grew up in a home where her parents yelled constantly – at one another, at her siblings, and at her. Often upset, tense, and powerless to change the situation, she grew to hate yelling. She would never be like that, she decided. She would never yell at her husband and children. When Evelyn grew up, married and had children, a surprising thing happened – she yelled just like her parents had. She hated it. She did not want to do it, but she could not seem to stop. It was like being in a nightmare, only she could not wake up. If people remarked that she resembled her mother, Evelyn became very upset.

Evelyn had formed a judgment against her parents: They were wrong to yell. She bound the judgment to herself with the vow not to repeat their unhealthy pattern. As an adult she found herself in bondage to her own judgment. It is sometimes said that when we point one finger at someone, our other three fingers are pointing back at us. Evelyn followed some simple steps to find freedom from her waking nightmare.

1. She acknowledged that she had broken the fifth commandment, *'Honor your father and your mother, so that you may live long in the land the Lord your God is giving you'* (Exodus 20:12). She repented of forming judgments against her parents and asked for God's forgiveness.

2. Evelyn confessed that she had judged her parents in the matter of their yelling, and she renounced the judgment in the name of Jesus. She declared her intention to exercise mercy in place of judgment.

3. She confessed her unrighteous vow never to be like her parents, and renounced it.

4. Evelyn forgave her parents for all their yelling, dealing individually with memorable instances.

5. Evelyn asked the Lord to show her other areas where she had judged her parents or failed to honor them. She prayed prayers of confession, repentance, and renunciation as God revealed new areas.

6. Evelyn made it a point to pray prayers of mercy, thanksgiving, and blessing when she prayed for her parents. She asked God to show her how to honor her parents.

The results were spectacular. Evelyn was gradually able to stop yelling at her husband and children. Her relationship with her parents, once strained and difficult, was transformed. Evelyn even received a personal 'thanksgiving' letter from her mother and was able to write one in return. New dimensions of mercy, love and blessing began to flow in their relationship. Now when people comment on the resemblance between mother and daughter, she smiles. *'Blessed are the merciful, for they will be shown mercy'* (Matthew 5:7).

Evelyn's experience was not an isolated one. She was one of a small group of intercessors who began to take the fifth commandment seriously. God taught the group how judgments bind and how freedom comes through choosing God's mercy in Christ. As a result, all these women and their families experienced new dimensions of freedom, healing and blessing. They also applied what they had learned to interceding for others. These intercessors, who had personally experienced both the bondage of judgment and the freedom of God's mercy, became very sensitive to the urgent need for mercy in the lives of others. Their personal experiences equipped them to compassionately and effectively extend God's mercy in prayer and in daily situations. As God's mercy has been multiplied, a widening circle of lives continues to be touched and changed.

There is an urgent need for us to learn to intercede with God's mercy in the body of Christ. We have long crippled ourselves and our brothers and sisters with judgments and criticism. Trying in our own strength to exercise wisdom and discernment, we are only now discovering that we have drunk the poison of criticism and have awakened in bondage to judgment.

> *'But the wisdom that comes from heaven is first of all pure; then peace-loving, considerate, submissive, full of mercy and good fruit, impartial and sincere. Peacemakers who sow in peace raise a harvest of righteousness.'*
> (James 3:17–18)

Let us turn to the Lord so we may find mercy and grace. Lord, deliver us from judgment. Lord, grant us your mercy!

> Father, thank you that *'in [your] great mercy [you] have given us new birth into a living hope through the resurrection of Jesus Christ from the dead, and into an inheritance that can never perish, spoil or fade'* (1 Peter 1:3–4). Thank you that your mercy triumphs over judgment. Your mercy endures forever. Lord, please teach me both to receive your mercy and to give it freely to others. Bring to light any judgments and vows that bind me. Please set me free and show me how to wield this powerful weapon of mercy as I intercede for others.

Love

> *'This is how we know what love is: Jesus Christ laid down his life for us. And we ought to lay down our lives for our brothers.'*
> (1 John 3:16)

Our world is full of confusion about love. Some people mistake infatuation for love. Others equate love with sex. Some believe love is an enthralling sensation which can evaporate as suddenly as it begins. To others love means intimacy. Still others see love as a fifty-fifty, give-and-take contract.

God understands our confusion. He knows our need and he has provided a way for us to know what love is – we must look at Jesus Christ. *'Greater love has no one than this, that one lay down his life for his friends'* (John 15:13). What a contrast to the love of this world! We naturally love only those who love us, and only when we feel like it or it is to our advantage.

Our flesh, together with the world and the devil, hates Jesus' definition of love. His love demands a commitment that is certain to cause us discomfort. It requires a faithfulness unto death. Can there be anything more abhorrent to our flesh?

How on earth can we love God's way? Only through the supernatural love of Jesus Christ living in us. It was Jesus' love which led him to the cross. It was love, not nails that held him there, and it was love that took him to the depths of the grave to taste death for every man. Jesus, with his greatest love, triumphed over death and the grave. This weapon of love is so powerful that, with it, Jesus defeated our most powerful and last enemy – death. These who love with the love of Jesus Christ need not fear loving even unto death.

1. Love Drives Out Fear

> *'And so we know and rely on the love God has for us. God is love. Whoever lives in love lives in God, and God in him. Love is made complete among us so that we will have confidence on the day of judgment, because in this world we are like him. There is no fear in love. But perfect love drives out fear, because fear has to do with punishment.'* (1 John 4:16–18)

Now here is an amazing thing – love drives out fear. Whether we care to admit it or not, we all struggle with fear. While individual experiences range from nagging worries that keep us awake to the full-blown terrors of death and judgment, fear is universal. We are afraid of everything – the future, pain, disaster, poverty, earthquakes, snakes, mice, war, one another – the list is endless. God understands this, and in the Bible he tells us not to be afraid more than three hundred times.

One of our greatest fears is rejection. We are deeply insecure. As children we fear the opinions of our peers and strive to gain acceptance. We will do almost anything – wear identical clothes, listen to the same music, and speak with the same slang. We grow from adolescents in bondage to uniformity into adults who strive to make our acceptance sure by impressive accomplishments, knowing the right people, being seen in the right places, and collecting the most sought-after possessions. We have everything and do everything, but we still fear rejection. As adults, we are no more secure than we were as adolescents. We may have made ourselves a bit more comfortable, but the basic roots of our insecurity remain.

What is our insecurity really about? All our fears are rooted in fear that God will reject us. This fear is rooted so deep that despite being told repeatedly that God loves us, the inside of us simply will not believe it. We need a deep solution to a deep problem.

This is what God provides: *'God is love ... perfect love drives out fear.'* God's solution is a deep revelation of himself – he wants to flood and overwhelm us with his love. This infilling of God's love, of his very presence, will eradicate our fear. Our fear is 'of punishment'. Flooded with God's love, acceptance and assurance, we do not fear punishment. Rather, God's matchless love produces in us confidence.

> *'If God is for us, who can be against us? He who did not spare his own Son, but gave him up for us all –*

> *how will he not also, along with him, graciously give*
> *us all things?'*   (Romans 8:31, 32)

Once we become partakers of God's matchless love and begin to know the holy confidence he provides, we can start to understand love as a spiritual weapon that drives out fear.

Mothers of small children understand how love drives out fear. Little Amy toddled along the park pathway a short distance from her mother. She was suddenly overtaken by a large dog. The dog stopped near the tiny child, fixed his gaze on a bird some distance ahead on the path, and let out a single bark. Little Amy's face contorted in terror. With an anguished wail, she made straight for her mother. Amy's mother picked her up, held her close and spoke with soothing words. In less than a minute Amy was smiling. A few minutes later she was again toddling confidently along the path. An earthly mother's love can eradicate fear and produce confidence. How much more the perfect love of our heavenly Father? Let us ask God to flood us with his love so we may demonstrate his love by our lives and actions.

> Merciful Father, I acknowledge that true love is found in you alone, for *'God is love.'* By your Spirit, please fill me with the love of your Son, Jesus Christ. Please flood my whole body, mind, soul and spirit with the knowledge of Christ Jesus, who laid down his life for me. May your love shine forth in my life and actions. Amen.

2. Love Subdues Our Enemies

With Jesus' love, we can love the unlovable and those who do not return our love. Jesus' love even enables us to love our enemies. To our worldly minds, this is ridiculous. We should fight fire with fire! How we need to remember that

God's weapons are far superior to anything the world has to offer. Love is God's weapon of choice for dealing with enemies.

> *'But I tell you who hear me: Love your enemies, do good to those who hate you, bless those who curse you, pray for those who mistreat you ... If you love those who love you, what credit is that to you? Even "sinners" love those who love them ... But love your enemies, do good to them, and lend to them without expecting to get anything back. Then your reward will be great, and you will be sons of the Most High, because he is kind to the ungrateful and wicked. Be merciful, just as your Father is merciful.'*
>
> (Luke 6:27, 32, 35–36)

Do not say, 'But you don't understand. My situation is different! These people don't respond to love; they only understand violence and vengeance.' Rather, trust God and obey his commands. Your own heart will be searched, tested, cleansed and healed, and you will receive a reward (Proverbs 25:21–22). You will also be set free to pray for your enemies according to God's heart and will. Love is the supreme weapon that Jesus used to rescue and save us. Let us not doubt its power or cast it aside. There is nothing Satan would like better. Let us allow Jesus fill us with his love and move us with his impulses.

3. Love Covers Sin

Love has another powerful feature as a spiritual weapon – it is able to cover sin. Peter says, *'Above all, love each other deeply, because love covers over a multitude of sins'* (1 Peter 4:8). But just how do we cover sin by loving one another? We need to know because there is a right way and a wrong way to cover sin.

A woman in full time Christian work, assigned to a new

department, soon realized her two supervisors were sexually involved. Other workers covered for them, making excuses and seeing they were not disturbed when they spent time alone. These workers did cover sin and probably did so out of affectionate solidarity, but they did not cover sin in the right way. How does God intend us to cover sin?

> 'Blessed is he
>   whose transgressions are forgiven,
>   whose sins are covered.
> Blessed is the man
>   whose sin the LORD does not count against him
>   and in whose spirit is no deceit.
> When I kept silent,
>   my bones wasted away
>   through my groaning all day long.
> For day and night
>   your hand was heavy upon me;
> my strength was sapped
>   as in the heart of summer.
> Then I acknowledged my sin to you
>   and did not cover up my iniquity.
> I said, "I will confess
>   my transgression to the LORD" –
> and you forgave
>   the guilt of my sin.'   (Psalm 32:1–5)

The one whose sins are covered is blessed. But the psalmist, David, says that when he covered up his sin, he was miserable. When he confessed it, willingly uncovering it before the Lord, the Lord forgave him and covered it. This is the way the Lord intends for us to cover sin.

In our fleshly love, we may feel that the best way to help our loved ones cover sin is to conspire with them to keep it hidden. But this allows our loved ones to continue the sinful behavior. It also means they cannot receive the kind of blessing David describes. Besides, conspiracy is a serious matter. The legal penalty for a crime complicated with conspiracy is usually greater than the same crime without it. In the spiritual realm, conspiracy to cover sin often lends strength to evil strongholds. When we keep sin covered this way, we deepen the darkness and strengthen the enemy's hand.

While we do not want to conspire to wrongly cover sin, neither do we want to see those we love shamed by its wholesale exposure. This can be very damaging and play into the enemy's favorite strategy of gossip and slander against God's people.

How can we exercise the love that covers sin? Most importantly, we can encourage one another to openly confess sin and repent.

Jane, the wife of a Christian leader, told me of her husband's unfaithfulness. She had told no one else. She was desperately upset and deeply embarrassed. Her husband, Craig, had revealed this only when he was confirmed to have contracted a sexually-transmitted disease. Craig was very ashamed of his behavior and upset over his failure to conquer sexual sin. Public exposure would certainly cause a scandal, damage the church, and ruin their careers. What could be done? How could I help?

1. One thing I did was to listen to Jane whenever she needed to talk. At that point, she had no one else with whom she could share. Jane needed someone she could trust to share her personal pain and struggle without fear of its becoming public.

2. Jane told Craig that she had shared their difficulty with me. Eventually we were able to meet and pray together. I encouraged them both to confess sin and to give and receive forgiveness. (Alternately, I could

have sought their permission to find them experienced and confidential spiritual help.)

3. I encouraged Craig to face the third party involved, to make a declaration of his determination to cease from sin, and to ask for forgiveness. (Were there an opportunity, it would also be desirable to try to help the other person involved to face the need for repentance, confession and receiving God's forgiveness.)

4. I strongly urged Craig and Jane to share their problem with their supervisor, pastor, or other authority to whom they were accountable. I encouraged them to set aside as much time as necessary for professional in-depth counselling. They did both these things. They left active Christian work for a time to address their problems at all levels. They received individual and joint counselling and rebuilt their marriage.

5. Craig and Jane also entered into relationships where they could be open and accountable for walking in the light. They now have others around them who know of their problems and can be vigilant on their behalf.

6. I prayed and interceded for them regularly. I stayed in relationship with Jane and Craig, not turning away because they had problems.

7. After their crisis had been resolved and they had returned to active Christian work, I continued to pray for them. I determined to speak up if I saw any 'danger signs' and to encourage them to deal with any future problems openly and promptly.

Jane and Craig experienced a full restoration of their marriage and ministries. Handling sin in this way brought it into the open before the people directly affected. It allowed for a right and godly covering of sin with love and forgiveness. It also involved those who to whom this couple were accountable. It respected their privacy while recognizing their need for accountability. It also made provision for help to address underlying problems.[3]

Most of the time when we need to deal with sin, the situation will not be a major one. It is frequently *'the little foxes that ruin the vineyards.'*[4] But these little things are just as destructive as the big emergencies. May we learn to deal with sin by uncovering it in the presence of our God who is Love so that we can receive an adequate and blessed covering for our sin.

> *'Brothers, if someone is caught in a sin, you who are spiritual should restore him gently. But watch yourself, or you also may be tempted. Carry each other's burdens, and in this way you will fulfill the law of Christ.'*
> (Galatians 6:1–2)

4. Acts of Intercession

> *'Dear children, let us not love with words or tongue but with actions and in truth.'* (1 John 3:18)

God sometimes allows me to have a personal involvement in the prayers he places in my heart. Usually this happens in little ways. For example, for about a year I had prayed regularly for a woman whom I had never met who had advanced breast cancer. One day I met her and had an opportunity to pray in her hearing the things I had been praying privately.

Occasionally there are opportunities of a larger scope. About six years ago God led my prayer partner, Carol, and me to begin praying about the unspeakable plight of unwanted children in China and Hong Kong. Soon our prayers included this entire generation of children. God blessed us with small glimpses into his wonderful plan for children. We prayed regularly and intensively for a several years.

Now both of our situations have changed. Carol and I rarely see each other or pray together. Neither of us has much time for concentrated intercession. Carol and her family are in the process of adopting a baby with developmental and health problems. Previously they provided foster care for a two-year-old girl with spina-bifida and a four-year-old boy with Down's Syndrome, both of whom are now enjoying new families in the US. My own family has expanded to include home schooling, an abandoned twelve year-old girl and our grand-daughter.

Have Carol and I stopped praying? Not at all. We think God is teaching us a different kind of prayer. The day came when God asked us to demonstrate in action what we had been praying with words. We had been asking him to rescue needy and helpless children and to let them experience his life, love and blessing. Then he placed needy children in front of us and asked, 'Do you really mean what you prayed? How much?'

What could we say? Part of me wanted to say, 'But God, you called me to intercede. How can I do any serious praying with so many children?' Then I remembered God's heart that I had come to know so well in those wonderful times of intercession and it was easy to say, 'Let the little children come.'

Acts of intercession are prayer in action. They are acts born out of the heart of God the Father and they bring powerful love and blessing into the lives of all involved, both givers and receivers.

> *'Be imitators of God, therefore, as dearly loved children and live a life of love, just as Christ loved us and gave himself up for us as a fragrant offering and sacrifice to God.'*   (Ephesians 5:1–2)

Father in heaven, I thank you for your matchless love demonstrated in the death and resurrection of your son Jesus Christ. Thank you for covering my sin with your love. Help me to always bring my sins to you, so I can receive your forgiveness and covering. Lord, please flood my life with your perfect love. Drive out all my fear and give me confidence of your acceptance. Teach me how to cover sin, bless my enemies and drive out fear with your love. Make me able to intercede for those who lack confidence, who are captive to sin, who are assailed by fears, who are imprisoned by fear of death, who live in terror of enemies or who fear punishment. May they be filled with your love. Make me sensitive to the leading of your Spirit to intercede with actions as well as with words.

Blessing

We know little about blessing today. I get the feeling that Isaac, Esau and Jacob knew a lot more about blessing than we do. When Isaac realized he had been tricked into blessing Jacob instead of firstborn Esau, Genesis 27:33 says he *'trembled violently'*. Isaac and Esau were not just angry at being tricked. Their greatest concern was the blessing itself.

> *'[Esau] burst out with a loud and bitter cry and said to his father, "Bless me – me too, my father! ... Haven't you reserved any blessing for me?"*
>
> *Isaac answered Esau, "I have made him lord over you and have made all his relatives his servants, and I have sustained him with grain and new wine. So what can I possibly do for you, my son?"*
>
> *Esau said to his father, "Do you have only one blessing, my father? Bless me too, my father!" Then Esau wept aloud.'*   (Genesis 27:33–38)

Unfortunately for Esau, Isaac's blessing of Jacob was so full and complete that there was little left for Esau. The stolen blessing caused a rift that took years to heal. Today, we think of receiving our father's blessing as synonymous with receiving his permission or consent. We do not consider it a thing of substance, a thing of value which could even be stolen. What have we been missing?

When the first man and woman disobeyed God, they and with them all mankind, fell from a place of blessing before God to one of cursing. (Compare Genesis 1:28 and 3:16–19.) Happily, this is not the end of the story. God promised that all the nations of the earth would be blessed through Abraham, the father of faith (Genesis 12:3).

Then God gave the law. And mankind said, 'Oh, good, all I have to do is keep these rules, and I'll be blessed.' The only trouble is, we cannot do it. The law is good and righteous, but try as we might, we cannot keep it perfectly, and so we find ourselves still under a curse. *'All who rely on observing the law are under a curse, for it is written: "Cursed is everyone who does not continue to do everything written in the Book of the Law"'* (Galatians 3:10). To avoid this curse of the law, we would have to keep every point of the law perfectly throughout our entire lives (James 2:10). The law cannot take us from curse to blessing, but faith in Jesus Christ can.

> *'Christ redeemed us from the curse of the law by becoming a curse for us, for it is written, "Cursed is everyone who is hung on a tree." He redeemed us in order that the blessing given to Abraham might come to the Gentiles through Christ Jesus.'*
>
> (Galatians 3:13–14)

We are critical thinkers who live in an age of criticism. We have been taught to question, challenge and criticize. We can debunk almost any argument. We know how to find flaws in the thinking, views and behavior of others. We study how to tear down, but we do not know how to build up. We know how to curse, but we have not learned how to bless.

'Now aren't you getting a little extreme? After all, we don't go around cursing people.' But we do, you know. We hardly consider the power of our words. God created the heavens and the earth by the word of his mouth (Hebrews 11:3; Psalm 33:6). His words are unimaginably powerful (Hebrews 4:12, 13). And God has created us in his image and has given us the power of speech (Genesis 1:26).

The Bible says that the tongue has the power of life and death (Proverbs 18:21), but we do not really believe it. If we did, these sentences and hundreds more like them would not sound so familiar:

'If you don't get to work, you'll never amount to anything.'

'He'll never make the grade.'

'I don't know what I ever saw in you.'

'You never help. You're really useless.'

'Can't you do anything right?'

'She really isn't very bright.'

'Drop dead.'

'Get lost.'

'He's just no good.'

'You'll never learn.'

'Go to hell.'

'With the tongue we praise our Lord and Father, and with it we curse men, who have been made in God's likeness. Out of the same mouth come praise and cursing. My brothers, this should not be.'

(James 3:9–10)

Now anyone who decides to quit cursing and start blessing will soon find the difficulty of it. Just as we cannot

158

seem to love God with our whole hearts and love our neighbors as ourselves, we also have trouble making the bitter stuff that comes out of our mouths sweet. But as with all of God's commands, he does not tell us to do something without providing the power to do it. He wants to change what comes out of our mouths at its source – in our hearts.

Just as faith in Christ Jesus moves us from curse to blessing with God, so also it can move us from curse to blessing with others. The basis for both receiving and giving blessing is through the blood of Jesus Christ. This truth is even reflected in the derivation of the English word 'to bless'. Webster's dictionary states that the word 'bless' comes from the Middle English word 'blessen' or 'bletsien', which comes from the Old English word 'bletsian' or 'bledsian', which in turn comes from the word 'blod', or 'blood'.[5] The blood of Jesus is the foundation of both receiving and giving blessing.

We have some wonderful opportunities to exercise God's command to bless. Every one of us who has been moved from curse to blessing through the blood of Jesus has the power, authority and responsibility to bless.

Whom are we to bless? Certainly anyone who has been an object of our criticism or cursing should now become an object of our blessing. An obvious place to begin is with our families. What about our relationship with our parents? Are there areas which have been characterized by our criticism or cursing? Let us allow God to transform our hearts and relationships as we replace cursing with blessing.

Parents have a wonderful opportunity to bless their children. Because God's blessings to us in Christ Jesus are unlimited, we have access to abundant blessing for each one of our children, whether we have one or twelve. Let us ask God to show us any ways in which we have been cursing rather than blessing our children. Let us ask God to make the bitter fountains of our hearts sweet. Let us ask him to teach us how to bestow blessing.

One thing some friends and I have found helpful has been to ask God to give us specific scriptures to use when praying for each family member. This has the wonderful effect of taking our eyes off problems and helping us to see glimpses of God's good plan for our loved ones. We can pray with a new sense of vision, authority and blessing.

Whom does God specifically tell us to bless? Our enemies. I think God knew we would have trouble believing and receiving this, so he repeated himself. May we learn to bless and inherit a blessing.

1. *'Bless those who persecute you; bless and do not curse.'*
   (Romans 12:14)

2. *'Blessed are those who are persecuted because of righteousness, for theirs is the kingdom of heaven. Blessed are you when people insult you, persecute you and falsely say all kinds of evil against you because of me. Rejoice and be glad, because great is your reward in heaven, for in the same way they persecuted the prophets who were before you.'* (Matthew 5: 10–12)

3. *'Do not repay evil with evil or insult with insult, but with blessing, because to this you were called so that you may inherit a blessing.'* (1 Peter 3:9)

Our blood-bought freedom to bless extends all the way to God's throne. It has always amazed and awed me that we are called to praise and bless God. The Hebrew word translated 'praise' in newer translations is often rendered 'bless' in the King James or Authorized Version.

'Bless the LORD, O my soul.' (Psalm 103:1 KJV)

'Praise the LORD, O my soul.' (Psalm 103:1 NIV)

When Jesus rode into Jerusalem before his arrest and crucifixion, he was greeted by crowds crying out praise and blessing. Jesus declared if they had been silent, the rocks would have cried out (Luke 19:40). *'They took palm branches and went out to meet him, shouting, "Hosanna!" "Blessed is he who comes in the name of the Lord!"'* (John 12:13). They cried out blessing and praise with the words of a prophetic psalm:

> *'O LORD, save us;*
> *O LORD, grant us success.*
> *Blessed is he who comes in the name of the LORD.*
> *From the house of the LORD we bless you.'*
>
> (Psalm 118:25–26)

Lord, you have freely given me your grace. You have given me blessing where without you I found only cursing. Reach into my heart and bring into your light all that causes me to curse when I should bless. Teach me to return blessing to those who have criticized or cursed me. Help me to bless so that I may inherit a blessing, through the grace of Jesus Christ. Amen.

Repentance and Confession

> *'... if my people, who are called by my name, will humble themselves and pray and seek my face and turn from their wicked ways, then will I hear from heaven and will forgive their sin and will heal their land.'*
>
> (2 Chronicles 7:14)

Intercession has certain qualities which make it distinctive from other types of prayer. Intercessors identify themselves with those for whom they pray. Intercessors often confess sin, repent and ask forgiveness on behalf of others. Intercession has a laying-down-one's-life quality. Of all our spiritual weapons, repentance and confession bear some of the deepest marks of these qualities. What does it take to step forward into the gap, to identify oneself with another to the point of identifying with his sin?

1. Personal relationship with God. '... *if my people, who are called by my name...* '
2. Humility. '... *will humble themselves...* '
3. Commitment to seek God. '... *and pray and seek my face...* '
4. Commitment to repent, confess and turn away from sin. '... *and turn from their wicked ways...* '

God promises that when we meet these conditions, he will hear, forgive and heal. In this scripture, God was calling his people to national repentance. Nations, however, are made up of individuals – individual hearts moved by God.

It is not to difficult to stand at an uninvolved distance and pray Pharisaical prayers for 'those people over there.' We have all done it. Yet God calls us to the intimate involvement of identification. Grief over sin then becomes real and personal, rather than a finger-pointing judgment-alism. What is our response when we see sin in our family, church, city or nation? Do we step back from personal involvement, or do we see ourselves as joined together with those for whom we pray? Do we pray with an 'us' and 'them' orientation, or do we include ourselves with humility and brokenness over sin.

Scripture contains examples of intercession which express this kind of identification. For example, when Ezra, a teacher of the law, came to Jerusalem from Babylon, he discovered that the Israelites there had intermarried with their pagan neighbors in disobedience to God's laws. Ezra was shocked, '*When I heard this, I tore my tunic and cloak, pulled hair from my head and beard and sat down appalled. Then everyone who trembled at the words of the God of Israel gathered around me because of this unfaithfulness of the exiles'* (Ezra 9:3–4). And Ezra prayed:

> *'O my God, I am too ashamed and disgraced to lift up my face to you, my God, because **our** sins are higher than **our** heads and **our** guilt has reached to the heavens. From the days of **our** forefathers until now, **our** guilt has been great. Because of our sins, **we** and **our** kings and **our** priests have been subjected to the sword and captivity, to pillage and humiliation at the hand of foreign kings, as it is today.'*
>
> (Ezra 9:6–7, emphasis mine)

Ezra, newly arrived in Jerusalem, had not married anyone and was not himself one of the 'unfaithful' exiles. Yet he did not pray for 'those people over there.' When he confessed sin and repented on behalf of his nation, he including himself. Ezra the law expert became Ezra the intercessor. He stepped into the rift, the place of broken fellowship, the place of sin. This was not merely an intellectual exercise, for the intercessor feels the weight of sin, he experiences sorrow over it, and he tastes the pain in God's heart concerning it.

The prayer of Daniel (Daniel 9:1–19) is another excellent example of intercessory repentance and confession of sin. (It also makes a useful outline for repentance.) This was not a casual 'quiet time.' His prayer was accompanied by Scripture reading, prayer, petition, fasting, sackcloth and ashes. Daniel confessed his own sin and the sin of his people. He repented of wickedness, rebellion, turning from God's commands, refusal to listen to God's servants and prophets, disobedience, not seeking God's favor and failure to turn from sin and heed the truth. He asked for restoration on the basis of God's mercy and purposes.

'We do not make requests of you because we are righteous, but because of your great mercy. O Lord, listen! O Lord, forgive! O Lord, hear and act! For your sake, O my God, do not delay, because your city and your people bear your Name.' (Daniel 9:18–19)

Moses

My favorite intercessor is Moses. He exhibited the laying-down-your-life quality of intercession better than anyone else in the Old Testament. Even after God's spectacular deliverance from Egypt through Moses, people were quick to grumble against him and blame him for every difficulty. When they complained about being hungry, God miraculously provided bread and meat. When were thirsty, they accused Moses of bringing them into the desert to die. *'Then Moses cried out to the LORD, "What am I to do with these people? They are almost ready to stone me"'* (Exodus 17:4). Poor Moses had not asked for this job. These were God's people, not his.

But as they went on through the desert, there was a change in Moses' attitude and a change in the way he prayed. This change seems directly related to Moses' deepening personal relationship with God.

The next recorded instance of Moses praying for the people is in Exodus 32. Moses had spent forty days and nights on Mount Sinai in God's presence. Moses' fellowship with God was interrupted by a crisis. The people, tired of waiting for Moses to reappear, had turned to idolatry. God told Moses,

'"Now leave me alone so that my anger may burn against them and I may destroy them. Then I will make you into a great nation.'

But Moses sought the favor of the LORD his God. "O LORD," he said, "why should your anger burn against

164

*your people, whom you brought up out of Egypt with
great power and a mighty hand? Why should the
Egyptians say, 'It was with evil intent that he brought
them out, to kill them in the mountains and to wipe
them off the face of the earth'? Turn from your fierce
anger; relent and do not bring disaster on your people.
Remember your servants Abraham, Isaac and Israel,
to whom you swore by your own self: 'I will make your
descendents as numerous as the stars in the sky and I
will give your descendants all this land I promised
them, and it will be their inheritance forever.'" Then
the* LORD *relented and did not bring on his people the
disaster he had threatened.'* (Exodus 32:10–14)

We can see a change in Moses' praying already. After
spending forty days and nights in uninterrupted fellowship
with God, Moses now had a better understanding of God's
plan and purposes. He knew more of God's heart. He
understood what God wanted to do for Israel. When God
said, *'Now leave me alone,'* Moses did not. He pleaded
with God according to his knowledge of God's plans and
promises. Moses interceded and God listened.

The next day, after confronting the people concerning
their idolatry, Moses again prayed for them. His prayer
now showed something of God's character. It had a laying-
down-your-life quality, *'Oh, what a great sin these people
have committed! They have made themselves gods of gold.
But now, please forgive their sin – but if not, then blot me
out of the book you have written'* (Exodus 32:31–32).
Moses placed himself in the gap.

Moses continued in close fellowship with God. He set
up a *'tent of meeting'* where, *'The* LORD *would speak to
Moses face to face, as a man speaks with his friend'* (Exodus
33:11). This close contact with God changed Moses'
attitudes, interests, and character. It changed the way

Moses prayed for himself. God's presence became more and more important to him.

> *'Moses said to the LORD, "You have been telling me, 'Lead these people,' but you have not let me know whom you will send with me. You have said, 'I know you by name and you have found favor with me.' If I have found favor in our eyes, teach me your ways so that I may know you and continue to find favor with you. Remember that this nation is your people."*
>
> *Then the LORD replied, "My Presence will go with you, and I will give you rest."*
> *Then Moses said to him, "If your Presence does not go with us, do not send us up from here. How will anyone know that you are pleased with me and with your people unless you go with us? What else will distinguish me and your people from all the other people on the face of the earth?"'*   (Exodus 33:12–16)

After this, Moses spent another forty days and nights with God. He witnessed God's glory and heard him proclaim his name. His inner transformation continued, and this is reflected in his prayers, *'O LORD, if I have found favor in your eyes,'* he said, *'then let the Lord go with us. Although this is a stiff-necked people, forgive our wickedness and our sin, and take us as your inheritance'* (Exodus 34:9). Moses was changed into someone who identified fully with God's people and purposes.

Moses reflects something of the character of Jesus who, *'poured out his life unto death, and was numbered with the transgressors. For he bore the sin of man, and made intercession for the transgressors'* (Isaiah 53:12). Jesus willingly and completely identified himself with us. *'God made him who had no sin to be sin for us, so that in him we*

might become the righteousness of God' (2 Corinthians
5:21).

Father, I see that these weapons of repentance and
confession can be mine only as I draw close to you
and remain in intimate fellowship with you. Pour out
your grace and mercy, and draw me to you. May I
*'always carry around in [my] body the death of Jesus,
so that the life of Jesus may also be revealed in [my]
body'* (2 Corinthians 4:10). Transform me by your
presence into one who identifies fully with those for
whom I pray. May I identify with your people,
desires, plans, promises, and purposes. May this be
what I express back to you in prayer.

Faith

*' "Have faith in God," Jesus answered. "I tell you the
truth, if anyone says to this mountain, 'Go, throw
yourself into the sea,' and does not doubt in his heart
but believes that what he says will happen, it will be
done for him. Therefore I tell you, whatever you ask for
in prayer, believe that you have received it, and it will
be yours." '*   (Mark 11:22–24)

We have already looked at faith as a defensive piece of
armor. Faith in Christ Jesus is also a powerful offensive
weapon which can overcome the world (1 John 5:4), effect
healing (Matthew 9:22), move mountains (Matthew 17:20–
21), open blind eyes (Luke 18:35–43), set the demonized
free (Matthew 15:21–28), and save (Luke 7:50).[6]

This faith is not something we drum up by 'positive
thinking' or by wishing extra hard, but it is given by the
Holy Spirit (1 Corinthians 12:9). We need to recognize
that we cannot produce faith through any amount of our
own effort, but like the man who brought his convulsing,

demonized son to Jesus, we need to cry to God for it. Jesus told the man, *"Everything is possible for him who believes." Immediately the boy's father exclaimed, "I do believe; help me overcome my unbelief"* (Mark 9:23–24).

Jesus was always interested in faith It was something he looked for, noticed and commented about. This should not really surprise us, since we know that *'... without faith it is impossible to please God, because anyone who comes to him must believe that he exists and that he rewards those who earnestly seek him'* (Hebrews 11:6).

Jesus expected his disciples to have faith and seemed surprised or distressed when they lacked it. When the disciples encountered a furious storm and cried out to Jesus to save them from drowning, he asked them, *'You of little faith, why are you so afraid?'* (Matthew 8:26). In Luke's account of the same incident, Jesus asked the disciples, *'Where is your faith?'* (Luke 8:25), as if they had left it somewhere or had misdirected it. When Peter began to sink while walking on the water, Jesus asked him, *'You of little faith ... why did you doubt?'* (Matthew 14:31). Jesus even connected lack of faith to the disciples' inability to understand spiritual words (Matthew 16:5–12). When Jesus visited his home town, he was unable to perform miracles, and *'he was amazed at their lack of faith'* (Mark 6:6).

Jesus looked for faith and encouraged people to put their trust in him, *'Trust in God; trust also in me'* (John 14:1). The problem comes when we somehow dislocate faith from the person of Jesus Christ. We try to understand or exercise faith in a vacuum. Faith that is not in Christ Jesus is not faith at all – it is just wishful thinking. This problem may be at the root of much of our disappointment about unanswered prayer.

Anna has been my friend for many years. Even though we come from vastly different cultures and usually think in different languages, I know her well. From years of friendship and working together, I know something of her character, priorities, desires and hopes. As a result, I trust her. I can speak openly and freely with her. I know she will continue to love and accept me. When Anna says she is going to do something, I can rest assured that she will do it. In a way, you see, I have faith in Anna. Looking at it this way, faith does not seem so elusive. The better we know God and the more we experience his grace and goodness, the stronger our faith becomes.

> Jesus, *'I do believe; help me overcome my unbelief.'* Thank you for your word which tells us that you did help this man believe, and his son was set free. Lord, like that man in your word, I choose to put my trust and confidence in you. I choose to believe your word, for *'faith comes from hearing the message, and the message is heard through the word of Christ'* (Romans 10:17). I believe *'that Christ died for our sins according to the Scriptures, that he was buried, that he was raised on the third day, according to the Scriptures'* (1 Corinthians 15:3-4). Lord, draw my heart after you, to seek you and to know you better. Lord help me to trust in you with my whole heart. May I not depend on my own understanding but acknowledge you in everything (Proverbs 3:5-6). Lord, give me a growing faith that I may become increasingly sure of what I hope for and certain of what I do not see (Hebrews 11:1).

Notes

1. *The Collins English Dictionary.* William Collins Sons & Co., Ltd., Glasgow, 1979, 1986, p. 965.
2. *Roget's II The New Thesaurus*, Expanded Edition. Houghton Mifflin Company, Boston, 1988, p. 636.

3. Suppose Craig had been unwilling to stop his sexually immoral behavior and had refused counsel, what then? Obviously, Jane would have needed support and friendship. Since Craig held responsibility in a position of Christian leadership, his actions would affect others spiritually. Jane and I could have considered asking Craig's supervisor or pastor to accompany us to try again. If a number of attempts like this had failed, Craig may have needed to be dealt with by the church (see Matthew 18:14-20). The goal of any such discipline should always be full restoration. For further reading, *Healing the Wounded*, by John White and Ken Blue, IVP, 1985, Leicester, deals extensively with church discipline.
4. Song of Songs 2:15.
5. *Webster's New World Dictionary of the American Language*, Second College Edition. World Publishing Company, 1980, p. 150.
6. For a list of things accomplished by faith, read Hebrews 11.

Chapter 6

Still More Weapons

Remembrance

> *'Only be careful, and watch yourselves closely so that you do not forget the things your eyes have seen or let them slip from your heart as long as you live. Teach them to your children and to their children after them.'*
> (Deuteronomy 4:9)

God rescued the entire nation of Israel from slavery in Egypt and led them to the land he had promised their forefathers. He gave them commandments and instructions to enable them to follow his ways and receive his promises. Moses exhorted the people to remember God, to remember his commands, to remember the Sabbath day, to remember what they had seen him do, to remember how God led them in the desert, to remember his mighty acts, and to continually speak to one another and to their children about these things. He frequently warned them about the danger of forgetting,

> *'When you have eaten and are satisfied, praise the LORD your God for the good land he has given you. Be careful that you do not forget the LORD your God, failing to observe his commands, his laws and his*

decrees that I am giving you this day. Otherwise, when you eat and are satisfied, when you build fine houses and settle down, and when your herds and flocks grow large and your silver and gold increase and all you have is multiplied, then your heart will become proud and you will forget the LORD your God, who brought you out of Egypt, out of the land of slavery.'

(Deuteronomy 8:10–14)

But Israel, like all of us, was forgetful. *'After that whole generation had been gathered to their fathers, another generation grew up, who knew neither the LORD nor what he had done for Israel. Then the Israelites did evil the eyes of the LORD and served the Baals. They forsook the LORD, the God of their fathers, who had brought them out of Egypt. They followed and worshiped various gods of the peoples around them'* (Judges 2:10–12). As a result, God caused them to be plundered and defeated by their enemies. As the sampling below suggests, forgetting can have serious consequences:

1. Idolatry, plundered and defeated by enemies (Judges 2:10–14).
2. Failure to wait for God's counsel (Psalm 106:9–13).
3. Pride, forgetting God, destruction (Deuteronomy 8:10–20).
4. Fear of enemies (Deuteronomy 7:17–19).
5. Making God angry and jealous (Deuteronomy 32:18–21).
6. Sin, rebellion, craving, willful demands, speaking against God (Psalm 78).

The New Testament is also full of exhortations to remember. The Apostle Peter emphasized this. *'Dear friends, this is now my second letter to you. I have written both of them as reminders to stimulate you to wholesome thinking. I want you to recall the words spoken in the past* by the holy prophets and the command given by our Lord and Savior through your apostles' (2 Peter 3:1–2). He has pointed out two things we should remember – the words of the prophets and the commands of Jesus. What are some of the other things scripture tells us to remember?

1. Remember the Lord. *'Remember Jesus Christ, raised from the dead, descended from David'* (2 Timothy 2:8).

2. Remember the death and resurrection of Jesus.

    "The Lord Jesus, on the night he was betrayed, took bread, and when he had given thanks, he broke it and said, "This is my body which is for you; do this in remembrance of me." In the same way, after supper he took the cup, saying, "This cup is the new covenant in my blood; do this, whenever you drink it, in remembrance of me."'

    (1 Corinthians 11:23–25)

3. Remember God's word. This will help protect us from sin, *'I have hidden your word in my heart that I might not sin against you'* (Psalm 119:11).

4. Remember the mighty things God has done, *'Remember the wonders he has done, his miracles, and the judgments he pronounced'* (Psalm 105:5).

5. Remember what God has done for us personally.

    'Praise the LORD, O my soul,
       and forget not all his benefits.
    He forgives all my sins
       and heals all my diseases;
    he redeems my life from the pit
       and crowns me with love and compassion.
    He satisfies my desires with good things
       so that my youth is renewed like the eagle's.'

    (Psalm 103:2–5)

6. *'Remember Lot's wife'* (Luke 17:32). Jesus exhorted us to remember this woman who was turned into a pillar of salt when she looked back to wicked Sodom as the Lord destroyed it (Genesis 19:26).

1. Memory Assistance

Some people object, 'You don't understand; I just can't remember scripture. I can't remember the verses, and I can't remember the references.' God, however, does understand. No one knows better than he just how forgetful we are. And he has provided 'memory assistance' for us through the Holy Spirit, *'All this I have spoken while still with you. But the Counselor, the Holy Spirit, whom the Father will send in my name, will teach you all things and will remind you of everything I have said to you'* (John 14:25–26). No memory? Then let us ask God to send his Holy Spirit upon us to make us able to remember.

People may think that those who can find just the right verse at the right time have fantastic memories. Maybe some do. More often, though, I think it is the Holy Spirit who has brought the verse to mind. I have a terrible memory, especially for names. (One time, while introducing my best friend, I finally had to ask her, 'What **is** your name?') Nevertheless, I am frequently able to remember the general contents and exact location of scriptures to address specific needs. Once, after becoming very excited about how the Lord had led me in this area, I tried to find the verses again so I could read them to my husband. When I was unable to remember or locate any of them again, I began to realize that this kind of 'remembering' has more to do with the Holy Spirit than with natural ability.

While the Holy Spirit is able to remind us of what God has said, it helps if we give him something to work with. We need to realize that he cannot remind us of something we have not heard! If we want the Holy Spirit to bring God's word to our minds, then we need to read it, meditate on it and talk about it. Let us fill our minds and hearts with God's word.

When we hear God speaking, it is important that we remember what he says so we can act on it. Some years ago, God renewed my relationship with him and suddenly I began to hear his voice more clearly. Delighted, I told my prayer partner, 'I think God must have talked to me for two hours this morning. His presence was so sweet.'

'That's great,' she answered, 'What did he say?'

Stunned, I answered, 'You know, I can't remember!' I promptly went out and bought an inexpensive notebook. In it I recorded what I sensed God saying. I also copied scriptures, recorded my prayers and God's answers, made Bible study notes and documented my fears, doubts, struggles with sins, and victories. Soon I expanded it to include notes from sermons. I discovered that when God spoke, he often repeated himself. While it was not always easy to know at first what to focus on, when ideas or scriptures started showing up in my notebook repeatedly, I started paying attention. Twenty-three notebooks later, I am continuing to try to listen to God, remember what he has said, and put it into practice. Remembrance helps me to stay on course and to avoid drifting, *'We must pay more careful attention, therefore, to what we have heard, so that we do not drift away'* (Hebrews 2:1).

In the time of Malachi, the people who heard and responded to God's message did something similar.

"Then those who feared the LORD talked with each other, and the LORD listened and heard. A scroll of remembrance was written in his presence concerning those who feared the LORD and honored his name.'
(Malachi 3:16)

2. Remembrance and Faith

I stood in the check-in line with a fistful of tickets and passports. We were returning to Hong Kong from the US. In just a few days, the children were to begin school, but we did not have enough money for their tuition. I fidgeted with the documents and looked around the terminal, half wondering if some stranger would give me an envelope. For the weeks we had been in the US we had been praying, asking God to provide. And now, empty-handed, we were about to board our return flight.

As we winged across the continental United States I prayed, 'God? Do you see us? We haven't got enough money to put the kids in school. What are you going to do?' As we flew I began to remember all the other times we had had no money and how each time, God had faithfully and graciously met our need.

I remembered the time we had searched for a place to live for a week. It poured with rain, while we drove here and there in our tiny car with two panting dogs, a toddler, and all the windows rolled up! By the end of a week we had spent our rent money on motels, food and gas. But at the last moment, God answered. He even made our remaining $70 enough to secure the lease.

I thought about all the times we had been down to our last few dollars, and God stepped in and met our needs in some unexpected way. I remembered all these times, slowly and deliberately, rehearsing them before the Lord. I realized, at that point, that God had faithfully taken care of us for ten years. Remembering and rehearsing the faithful provision of God in the past gave me strength and courage to trust him to meet our present needs.

We landed on the West coast to change flights. Our former pastor and his wife came to meet my husband,

Casey, who would stay in the US for a few more weeks. But no one gave us anything.

The children and I said goodbye, passed through the security check and headed for the boarding area. The departure area was crowded, noisy and chaotic. The airline had apparently overlooked a Chinese holiday, and the flight was severely overbooked. Airline officials were inviting passengers with no pressing engagements to disembark and travel the following day. They offered cash compensation, accommodation, meals, travel and confirmed seats on the next day's flight. We accepted their gracious offer. The next day they asked if we would be willing to stay a second day, amounting to double compensation. We rested again in a comfortable hotel. On the third day, clutching my boarding passes, I was summoned to the gate desk. The official tore up our boarding passes and issued us new ones – for business class. We returned to Hong Kong rested, relaxed, with enough money not only for school, but also to live on for several months.

When I cannot see how we will buy groceries next week, I remember God's faithfulness. This exercise of the weapon of remembrance strengthens and releases faith to trust God for our needs.

This weapon is especially helpful is when praying for people with incurable illnesses. Rather than focusing on the condition or hopeless prognosis, we can choose to remember incidents of God's healing. Recently I have been praying with a lady who suffers from rheumatoid arthritis. I know arthritis is incurable and relentlessly destructive, but I also know another lady who has been completely and permanently healed of arthritis by God. When I pray, this is what I remember before God. I rehearse the details; I tell the story. Remembrance strengthens my faith so I can dare to ask God for the impossible.

Scripture provides a wealth of great deeds and mighty acts we can remember. There are also plenty of contemporary 'books of remembrance' available. Christian book stores generally have a whole section devoted to testimonies and biographies.

David frequently used remembrance as a spiritual weapon. The Psalms are filled with examples. In Psalm 77, Asaph the psalmist, was having a faith crisis.

> 'Will the LORD reject forever?
>   Will he never show his favor again?
> Has his unfailing love vanished forever?
>   Has his promise failed for all time?
> Has God forgotten to be merciful?
>   Has he in anger withheld his compassion?'
>
> (Psalm 77:7–9)

Asaph decided to trust God.

> 'I will remember the deeds of the LORD;
>   yes, I will remember your miracles of long ago.
> I will meditate on all your works
>   and consider all your mighty deeds.'
>
> (Psalm 77:11–12)

Then he recounted Israel's amazing deliverance from Egypt. Asaph, in the face of impossible circumstances, chose to cry out to God and remember his promises, faithfulness, and mighty acts.

3. Remembrance and Healing

As a student psychiatric nurse, I was asked to reveal my earliest memory. I tried to avoid answering and finally recounted a much later memory. I was unwilling to divulge my early memories for analysis because they were all negative incidents linked to resentment. They involved someone thwarting my desires, failing to meet my needs, or

humiliating me. I did not seem to have any happy
memories before age eight or nine. The psychologists and
my classmates would have had a picnic!

I had been raised in a fairly normal, loving family, so
why were my memories were so negative? After I turned
my life over to Jesus, God began the process of healing me
from the inside out. He gently uncovered layers of
bitterness, anger and resentment and graciously covered
me with his grace and forgiveness. In prayer, he sometimes
led me to remember some painful incident in his presence.
He led me to forgive and release those whom I had held in
resentment and bitter anger. I was surprised to find that
my 'baby' emotions had adult strength. As God gradually
healed my past, an unexpected thing happened. I began to
remember things from my early years – and they were
happy memories. My old, unhappy memories, no longer
empowered by bitterness and resentment, faded into the
background. These experiences have helped me to understand that a great deal of what we remember and forget is
by choice. As we yield ourselves to God, he heals us by
his Spirit and gives us renewed minds and wholesome
memories.

> *'Therefore, I urge you, brothers, in view of God's
> mercy, to offer your bodies as living sacrifices, holy and
> pleasing to God – which is your spiritual worship. Do
> not conform any longer to the pattern of this world, but
> be transformed by the renewing of your mind. Then
> you will be able to test and approve what God's will is
> – his good, pleasing and perfect will.'*
>
> (Romans 12:1–2)

4. Remembrance and the Next Generation

Remembrance acts as a weapon to protect, train and
prepare the next generation. I have sometimes heard it

said that God has no grandchildren. Certainly this is true, since God intends each one of us to become his own dear child, '... *to all who received him, to those who believed in his name, he gave the right to become children of God – children born not of natural descent, nor of human decision or a husband's will, but born of God'* (John 1:12–13).

Yet in our churches we do have God's grandchildren – people who attend church because their parents did. They are second, third or fourth generation Christians. They are culturally Christian, but they lack a personal relationship with God.

Israel had the same problem. That is why God wanted the memory of his mighty works and commandments to be passed from one generation to the next. The consistent, faithful exercise of remembrance was meant to give the next generation a factual, historical, spiritual heritage, creating in them a personal desire to know and follow God.

> *'Love the LORD your God with all your heart and all your soul and all your strength. These commandments that I give to you today are to be upon your hearts. Impress them on your children. Talk about them when you sit at home and when you walk along the road, when you lie down and when you get up.'*
>
> (Deuteronomy 6:5–7)

Careful teaching and training helps insure that the next generation will seek and follow the Lord. Instructed in the facts of our faith and trained in holy living, our children will receive a measure of protection from the strong pull of the pagan world which surrounds us. They will learn how to call upon the Lord. This is the best foundation we can give them as they move from dependence on us to responsibility towards God (Proverbs 22:6).

Father, I give you my body, my whole life – past, present and future. I yield my memory to you, recognizing that it is you who created me with the capacity for memory and self-consciousness. Jesus, I invite you to be Lord of my memory – to cleanse, heal and use it for your glory. Holy Spirit, remind me of all God has said. Give me a hunger and thirst for God's word and anoint me to remember what I read and hear.

Enable me to use remembrance as a weapon in prayer and intercession. Grant me opportunities to 'remember' in my children's and grandchildren's hearing, your faithfulness and goodness, your power and mighty acts. May the next generation be planted firmly and may they build upon the good foundations of faith you have provided in Christ Jesus. Amen.

Binding and Loosing

'In fact, no one can enter a strong man's house and carry off his possessions unless he first ties up the strong man. Then he can rob his house.'

(Mark 3:27)

The strong man is Satan, and the one who ties him up is Jesus. God intends that, in Christ Jesus, we will overcome Satan, win back territory for God, and set free those whom Satan has held captive. Let us remember that Jesus Christ has already overcome Satan. All that remains is for us to do is to exercise faith in what Jesus has done. In this invisible war in the spiritual realms, we are to enter the strong man's house, bind him, and take back what he has stolen. Before we decide to retreat in panic, let us look a little more closely at the authority Jesus Christ has given us to bind and loose.

a little more closely at the authority Jesus Christ has given us to bind and loose.

> ' "But what about you?" he asked, "Who do you say I am?"
>
> Simon Peter answered, "You are the Christ, the Son of the living God."
>
> Jesus replied, "Blessed are you, Simon son of Jonah, for this was not revealed to you by man, but by my Father in heaven. And I tell you that you are Peter, and on this rock I will build my church, and the gates of Hades will not overcome it. I will give you the keys of the kingdom of heaven; whatever you bind on earth will be bound in heaven, and whatever you loose on earth will be loosed in heaven." Then he warned his disciples not to tell anyone he was the Christ.'
>
> (Matthew 16:15–20)

Jesus said he would give Peter the keys of the kingdom of heaven. Apparently these keys were related to Peter's recognition and confession of Jesus as the Christ. The important distinction here is that Peter recognized Jesus by revelation from the Father, not because someone else told him. Those who recognize Jesus by revelation are the believers that Hades cannot overcome. This is the church with the keys – with the power and authority to bind and loose.

Part of the church's fear and inability to confront and bind the strong man rests here. Too many of us know who Jesus is only because someone else has told us. Not enough of us have sought the Father for a revelation of Jesus Christ. This is what we need, individually and collectively. Then the church will wield kingdom-of-heaven power and authority.

In any area where we see Satan possessing or influencing that which rightfully belongs to God, we may pray in the power and authority of Jesus' name to bind or restrain him. The same can be done with any troublesome spirit. When this simple prayer is combined with faith based on a revelation of Jesus Christ, the power and authority of Christ's victory comes against Satan and he is restrained.

1. Plundering the Strong Man's House

Just as we have authority to bind Satan and his minions, we can also release all that Satan has bound. Christians suffer from many kinds of bondage, but release is available in Christ Jesus. Although we are talking about these things in the context of prayer, release may require action. Complete and permanent release may require lifestyle changes. What are some of the things we may need to be released from? A short tour of Scripture will give us some ideas.

1. **Debt** (Deuteronomy 15:1–6). God had arranged for his people to be free from poverty and debt. His plan included the complete cancellation of all debt every seventh year. Today many Christians are bound by debt. Debts easily snowball out of control. Debt frequently prevents Christians from responding to God's call to missions. They hear God's call and want to respond, but they cannot because of financial commitments.

2. **Slavery** (Deuteronomy 15:12–14). In Bible times, when a man had nothing left and could not eat, he sold himself and his family as slaves. God intended his people to be free, so he limited the term of slavery to six years. The seventh year all slaves had to be set free and generously supplied with food and clothes. While in most western countries slavery has been abolished, it may take variant forms. I once saw a television documentary about a jazz musician whose manager had cheated him. Pretending to pay the

money, with interest. So at age seventy-five, he still must perform every day of the year. Except for a small stipend to meet his daily needs, everything he earns goes to the government. Unfortunately, the compounding interest on his delinquent taxes exceeds the money he can earn, so his debt continues to grow. Unless the government forgives his debt, this old, black musician will go to his grave a slave.

In many places in Asia indentured servitude or outright slavery is common. The poor sell themselves or their children into slavery because they have no other way to survive. While they may theoretically have the opportunity for release, relentless economic pressures make them permanent slaves.

We have been talking here about economic slavery, but many of us are also slaves to habits. Most of us have probably forgotten the first time we gave way to that impulse. But the next time it was easier. Soon we were firmly in the grip of a bad habit, slaves to our own evil impulses.

3. **Oaths or curses** (Numbers 30:2, Acts 23:12ff).

> *'But I say to you, Do not swear at all ... Simply let your "Yes" be "Yes", and your "No", "No"; anything beyond this comes from the evil one.'*
>
> (Matthew 5:34, 37)

Oblivious to Jesus' admonition, many of us bind ourselves and others with oaths and curses. We say things like, 'If there's one thing I'll never do, it's ...,' 'I wouldn't be caught dead ...,' and 'Over my dead body!' without even thinking about the meaning or power of our words.

Many years ago I said, 'If there's one place I will never go, it's Southeast Asia.' At this writing, I have lived in Hong Kong for fifteen years! What happened? I used to think that when God heard such oaths, he took up the challenge and arranged for me to do the thing I was unwilling to do. Now that I know him better, I realize I was wrong. God is good, and what he does is good (Psalm 119:68). He has good plans for each of us (Jeremiah 29:11–13). Now I suspect it was really Satan who incited me to utter oaths that were contrary to God's good plan for my life.

Below are some more things mentioned in the Bible from which people needed to be released.

4. **Prison** (Psalm 107:10–16, 102:20; Acts 12:6–7).
5. **Death** (Psalm 107:18–20; John 11:43–44).
6. **Foolishness** (Proverbs 22:15).
7. **Religious heavy burdens** (Matthew 23:4).
8. **The Law** (Galatians 4:21–31, 5:1).
9. **Affliction** (Psalm 107:17; Isaiah 53:4).
10. **Sin** (Proverbs 5:22).
11. **Crippling handicap** (Luke 13:16).
12. **Opposing the Lord's servant** (2 Timothy 2:24–26).

2. Binding Up the Broken-Hearted

'The Spirit of the Sovereign LORD is on me, because the LORD has anointed me to preach good news to the poor. He has sent me to bind up the broken-hearted . . .'

(Isaiah 61:1)

'Come, let us return to the LORD. He has torn us to pieces but he will heal us; he has injured us but he will bind up our wounds.' (Hosea 6:1)

Through Christ, we can bind up the broken-hearted and those who have been wounded. There is probably no ministry more needed in the body of Christ today. Our churches are full of wounded and broken-hearted people.

We have preached the gospel to people; we have told people how to believe in Jesus; we have baptized them and taught them to attend church, pray, and read their Bibles. We preach them sermons and tabulate their numbers. But all too often we do little or nothing to bind up the wounded among us.

People are sometimes seriously wounded **in** the church, by other Christians. Many of us do not have too much trouble forgiving non-Christians – they don't know any better. But it can be difficult to forgive and receive healing for wounds inflicted by other believers.

At times all of us need a personal touch of God's love, compassion, and healing ministered by another through prayer. The wounded among us are especially needy. Some wounded Christians wander from church to church, searching for God's healing touch. Others suffer quietly, becoming distant and indifferent. Some go back to the world, not so much giving up on the Lord as giving up on the church.

Who are the wounded or wandering Christians you know? Why not begin now to intercede regularly for one or two of them? Ask the Lord to show you ways to bring them a word of encouragement or a touch of love. The Spirit of the Sovereign Lord will come upon you, anointing you to preach the good news to the poor and bind up the broken-hearted.

> Lord Jesus, I rejoice because you have already disarmed all the powers and authorities of the evil one and have made a public spectacle of them, triumphing over them by your cross (Colossians 2:15). I rejoice, Lord, that you have given those who know you power and authority to overcome all the power of the enemy – to bind the evil one and plunder his house.

In Jesus' name I bind every deceptive or lying spirit of the enemy, every blinding or hindering spirit and every complacent spirit which would seek to rob me and others in the body of Christ of a full complete personal revelation of Jesus Christ. Father, by your Spirit please grant us an urgent desire to seek you wholeheartedly.

Father, I ask you to give me a revelation of the Lord Jesus Christ, that I will know him because you have shown him to me, not only because of what others have said about him. Father, I need an on-going revelation of your Son Jesus, not just one from long ago.

Sovereign Lord, please send your Spirit upon us, anointing us to preach good news to the poor and to bind up the broken-hearted. Lead me to those who are wounded and discouraged. May your Spirit work through me to bind them up and bring them healing.

Tearing Down and Building Up, Uprooting and Planting

'And it will be said, "Build up, build up, prepare the road! Remove the obstacles out of the way of my people." For this is what the high and lofty One says – he who lives forever, whose name is holy; "I live in a high and holy place, but also with him who is contrite and lowly in spirit..."'

(Isaiah 57:14–15)

'Since you are eager to have spiritual gifts, try to excel in gifts that build up the church.'

(1 Corinthians 14:12)

It is much easier to tear down than to build up. Our nations are full of revolutionaries, eager to tear down governments, but few can be found who have the vision, wisdom and skill to build. Anyone can see what is wrong, but few know how to fix it.

Suppose we have a shed that we want torn down. Whom shall we hire? Any strong, willing worker will do. He needs no particular skill. But whom shall we hire to build a new structure? Now we become more careful. We make inquiries and check listings of approved contractors. We hire the most experienced, reputable, and skilled contractor we can afford. We know that construction is not as easy as demolition.

Anyone can tear down, but building up takes wisdom, knowledge and skill. God calls us to excel in the gifts that build up others, that build up the church. Many of us are skilled at criticism and finding fault. We are good at it in prayer, too. We cast down and rebuke. We pray against this and that. But God has designed tearing down and building up, and uprooting and planting as weapon pairs. Let me illustrate.

In my home town, there is an abandoned house. Over many years, it has become so dilapidated that it is nothing but a standing ruin, useless and decrepit beyond repair. Yet no one has bothered to tear it down. No doubt it will stay there until someone decides to build on that site.

It is the same with gardens. We have all seen a garden overgrown with weeds. When we see that someone has uprooted and cleared away the weeds, we get interested. Each time we pass by we check on the progress. Will the gardener plant flowers or vegetables? We look expectantly because we know that no one bothers to pull up weeds unless he intends to plant something.

Likewise, in prayer, the one who tears down must do so only to build up. The one who uproots must have something to plant. Tearing down or uprooting for any other reason is useless and destructive. When we take up potentially destructive weapons in prayer, let us be very careful, lest we find ourselves partners with the one who destroys (John 10:10).

It is very easy to pray tearing down and uprooting prayers out of our own hurt and bitterness. May God forgive us for prayers designed to tear down and uproot when we had no intention of building or planting. When we pray, let us ask God first to search our hearts. May he uproot bitterness and tear down any wicked thing that exalts itself against the knowledge of God. *'Wisdom is better than weapons of war, but one sinner destroys much good'* (Ecclesiastes 9:18).

God's word tells us that there is a proper time for everything, including uprooting and tearing down, and planting and building (Ecclesiastes 3:2–3). May the Lord give us discernment, so we can understand his times and purposes in our lives and in the lives of those for whom we pray (Matthew 16:2–3).

Some uprooting is not our business. God himself will take care of it at the time he has set (Matthew 13:27–30). If we are in doubt about whether to tear down, let us leave it for the time being. May we concentrate rather on how to build and plant.

Nehemiah and His Warrior Builders

The book of Nehemiah presents a graphic picture of building in times of war. A small band of exiled Israelites had already been back in the land for many years. They had rebuilt the temple and reinstituted worship there. People worked very hard, but the walls of the city remained broken down. Rubble was everywhere. They frequently came under attack as their enemies tried to prevent them from restoring the city. Chapters 3 and 4 of

Nehemiah outline a strategy useful to today's spiritual warriors who seek to build up the body of Christ through prayer. (It will be helpful to read Nehemiah 3 and 4 before continuing.)

1. People worked on the whole wall at once, making repairs in their immediate neighborhoods (Nehemiah 3). Similarly, those who pray will do so where they are, concentrating especially on their local situation. As each worker on the wall was involved because he shared the vision to rebuild the walls of Jerusalem, so each intercessor prays because he has a vision of God's plan and purpose for the church.

2. The work seemed hopeless and impossible. God sent Nehemiah who provided vision, leadership and strategy. God will provide prayer leaders with vision and strategy for intercession today.

3. When threatened by the enemy, the people prayed to God (Nehemiah 4:1–5). When we meet spiritual opposition in prayer today, our first response must be to turn to God.

4. When threatened with attack, they posted guards around the clock (Nehemiah 4:9). Nehemiah understood the threat of enemy attack and devised an effective strategy to meet it. As we build the body of Christ, we must not be unaware of the enemy and his schemes (2 Corinthians 2:11). Like the builders of Jerusalem, we will certainly meet spiritual opposition. We need to learn effective strategies for prayer and spiritual warfare in our specific situations.

5. At the lowest places in the wall, Nehemiah posted people in family groups with swords, spears and bows (Nehemiah 4:13). The family unit is God's design. We must do everything we can to respect and support the integrity of our families. Yet in our churches we may inadvertently undermine family life by separating

family members according to age or by designing activities for 'adults only'. We need to understand that the family is our most basic defense against the isolation that leads to spiritual ruin (Psalm 68:6).

6. The people became exhausted and discouraged because there was so much rubble that they could not rebuild the wall. Nehemiah provided encouragement and reminded them what was at stake, *'Don't be afraid of them. Remember the Lord, who is great and awesome, and fight for your brothers, your sons, and your daughters, your wives and your homes'* (Nehemiah 4:14). In our day, let us ask God to give us the ability to help and encourage one another.

7. When Israel's enemies realized that the wall was being built in spite of their threats and schemes, their attack became more intense. Work then went forward with half the people standing guard and the others building. The builders were prepared for attack, *'Those who carried materials did their work with one hand and held a weapon in the other, and each of the builders wore his sword at his side as he worked'* (Nehemiah 4:17–18).

The entire city was on a war footing, and everyone slept fully dressed and armed (Nehemiah 4:16–23). Similarly, as we choose to press ahead building up the body of Christ in prayer, we will find ourselves under spiritual pressure. Each step forward will be contested. It will be necessary for us to give up our comfortable lifestyle and move our whole lives to a wartime footing characterized by watchfulness, instant obedience and sacrifice.

8. Some people acted as watchmen and Nehemiah arranged a communication system so everyone could be instantly alerted in case of attack. Today God is

raising up watchmen and establishing communication among intercessors worldwide. When one area comes under focused attack, the call will go out for prayer reinforcements.

9. Despite all kinds of physical, psychological and political opposition, the wall of Jerusalem was restored. *'When all our enemies heard about this and all the surrounding nations saw it, our enemies were afraid and lost their self-confidence, because they realized that this work had been done with the help of our God'* (Nehemiah 6:16). As we move ahead in obedient prayer, fully committed to seeing God's plans and purposes accomplished, God himself will work through us and the body of Christ will be built up. This will act as a testimony and the nations will fear the Lord (Psalm 46).

Heavenly Father, I thank you for the weapons you have placed in my hands to tear down and uproot, and to build and plant. I invite you to search my heart and uproot any bitterness you find there. Free me to pray according to the leading of your Spirit rather than out of hurt or bitterness. Enable me to discern your plans and purposes, so I will know when to tear down and how to build up. Lord, teach me to be a builder and a planter. Father, give me vision to see the unity Jesus Christ died to secure for us. Show me how to build and battle in the place on the wall you have assigned to me. In Jesus' name, teach me how to pray.

Thanksgiving

'Be joyful always; pray continually, give thanks in all circumstances, for this is God's will for you in Christ Jesus.'   (1 Thessalonians 5:16–18)

> *'I urge, then, first of all, that requests, prayers, intercession and thanksgiving be made for everyone...'*   (1 Timothy 2:1)

> *'Do not be anxious about anything, but in everything, by prayer and petition, with thanksgiving, present your requests to God.'*   (Philippians 4:6)

Even a cursory survey of the Bible reveals that God intends our prayers to abound with thanksgiving. Obviously we want to give God thanks for his blessings and the good things he gives us, but how can we thank God **'for everything'**, **'for everyone'** and **'in all circumstances'**? Is it really God's will for me to give thanks when my friend has brain cancer, when my child has rejected God, or when someone has been cruel to me? Is God some kind of sadistic, egotistical despot who likes to see us grovel?

It really **is** God's will for us to give thanks in every situation, the bad as well as the good. God is neither egotistical nor sadistic. God is good and what he does is good (Psalm 119:68; Mark 10:18). Far from being untouched by our suffering, he has experienced it all personally (Hebrews 4:15; Isaiah 53:4–11). He is the one who cares so much he died for us on the cross (Romans 5:8). God has no need to authenticate his position as God by exercising perverse power over us like some petty emperor. And he certainly derives no pleasure from our pain and distress (Isaiah 63:9). Why, then, does God ask us to give thanks in all circumstances? The answer lies not so much in the nature of our circumstances as in the nature of God. *'Give thanks to the LORD, for he is good; his love endures forever'* (Psalm 118:1). Regardless of our own situation, we can choose to give God thanks in recognition that he is eternally loving and good. God commands us to give thanks to help lift up our eyes beyond the limited and sometimes crippling scope of our own circumstances. He invites us to lift up our eyes and focus on him. And when we obey him, our whole perspective changes.

Spiritual warfare is waged primarily in the realm of our minds. It is here we first experience victory or taste defeat. Giving thanks can break that all too familiar downward spiral of thinking which can begin when any little thing goes wrong. We start with a little complaining and end up firmly rooted in bitterness, drowning in self-pity, and convinced that God is not good at all. Turning to God with an offering of thanks is sometimes all that is needed to lift us out of our mental pit and turn defeat into victory.

When we are having difficulty finding things for which to thank God, Scripture gives plenty of suggestions. Here are a few of them:

1. God's unfailing love and wonderful deeds (Psalm 107:21-22).
2. God's righteous laws (Psalm 119:62).
3. God's provision (Mark 8:7; 2 Corinthians 9:10-11).
4. God's revelation (Daniel 2:23).
5. Jesus Christ (Luke 2:38).
6. God's near name (Psalm 75:1).
7. Salvation (Colossians 1:12-14).
8. The Lord's supper (Luke 22:17-19).
9. God's rule and reign (Revelation 4:9, 7:12, 11:17).
10. Victory (2 Corinthians 2:14; 1 Corinthians 15:57).
11. One another (Ephesians 1:16; Colossians 1:3-4; 1 Timothy 2:1; 2 Thessalonians 2:13).
12. See Psalm 136.

Thanksgiving can be a powerful weapon against a range of nasty things in our thought lives and personal relationships. It can defend us against the ingratitude and complaining which lead to rebellion.

Only weeks after God delivered the Israelites from the slavery of Egypt, we find them in the desert grumbling against their leaders, *'If only we had died by the LORD's hand in Egypt! There we sat around pots of meat and ate all the food we wanted, but you have brought us out into this desert to starve this entire assembly to death'* (Exodus 16:3). Apparently, thanksgiving for their deliverance evaporated in the desert as they began to grumble. God had met their needs, miraculously providing food and water. Even their clothes and shoes did not wear out. Yet none of this delivered them from complaining. Their grumbling soon led them to oppose God's appointed leaders. They ended up in rebellion and death (Numbers 11–21).

Giving thanks is also a cure for foolish talk. Among God's people there should not *be obscenity, foolish talk or coarse joking, which are out of place, but rather thanksgiving'* (Ephesians 5:4).

In Romans, Paul lists the grievous consequences of refusing to give thanks and acknowledge God,

> *'For although they knew God, they neither glorified him as God nor gave thanks to him, but their thinking became futile and their foolish hearts were darkened. Although they claimed to be wise, they became fools and exchanged the glory of the immortal God for images made to look like mortal man and birds and animals and reptiles.'* (Romans 1:21–23)

Prayer with thanksgiving is also God's prescription for anxiety.

> *'Do not be anxious about anything, but in everything, by prayer and petition, with thanksgiving, present your requests to God. And the peace of God, which transcends all understanding, will guard your hearts and your minds in Christ Jesus.'* (Philippians 4:6–7)

When used together with weapons such as praise, faith, remembrance and God's word, thanksgiving is a powerful prayer weapon. Thanksgiving is a characteristic of God's restored people (Isaiah 51:3; Colossians 3:15) and life in heaven (Revelation 7:12).

There are many times when my attitude is anything but thankful. With my grumbling, complaining heart, I drag into church. But I find that once I stop grumbling and come into God's presence with thanksgiving, my attitude is transformed. In his grace God restores me and gives me a glimpse of his glory. I go home a different person.

Coming into God's Presence

'Enter his gates with thanksgiving
and his courts with praise;
give thanks to him and praise his name.
For the LORD is good and his love endures forever;
his faithfulness continues through all generations.'
(Psalm 100:4–5)

How do we give thanks to God? First of all, God does not want us to come into his presence empty-handed. We are to bring thanksgiving and praise. God says the gates of Zion are named Praise (Isaiah 60:18). I wonder whether we can really come into his presence without thanksgiving and praise.

If we do not know how to bring thanksgiving to God, the Bible is full of helpful information and commands. We can give him thanks anytime, even when we wake up in the middle of the night (Psalm 119:62). We can give him thanks on a regular basis in our private prayer times, as Daniel did three times a day (Daniel 6:10). We can give God thanks in public worship gatherings (Psalm 35:18). Scripture frequently mentions thanksgiving in connection with music and song.

'Let us come before him with thanksgiving
and extol him with music and song.'
(Psalm 95:2)

'Sing unto the LORD with thanksgiving;
make music to our God on the harp.'
(Psalm 147:7)

Father God, please forgive me for all the times I have come into your presence with complaining, making requests born out of dissatisfaction. Change me into someone whose prayers are filled with thanksgiving and praise. Forgive me for failing to thank you for your goodness, mercy, and holiness. I thank you especially for your free salvation through Christ Jesus.

Forgive me for all the times I have grumbled and complained against others rather than giving you thanks for them. Grant me a heart filled with your grace to give you thanks at all times for all people and in all circumstances. Help me Lord, and *'I will praise God's name in song, and glorify him with thanksgiving'* (Psalm 69:30).

Revelation 12:11

'They overcame him by the blood of the Lamb and by the word of their testimony; they did not love their lives so much as to shrink from death.' (Revelation 12:11)

Revelation 12:11 presents a spiritual weapons group. While each is strong individually, together they are powerful enough to overcome Satan himself. They deserve a closer look.

1. The Blood of the Lamb

This Lamb, Jesus Christ, *'who takes away the sin of the*

world,' was publicly introduced just after his baptism by John the Baptist (John 1:29). But this is not the only place in the Bible where we find the Lamb. Lambs, blood and the remission of sin form a major theme of Scripture.

God testifies that, *'all have sinned and fall short of the glory of God'* (Romans 3:23). The Bible plainly teaches that the person who sins will die (Ezekiel 18:4; Romans 5:12). Since sin causes death, we humans desperately need to get rid of it.

God says that *'without the shedding of blood there is no forgiveness'* (Hebrews 9:22). Under the Old Covenant, God set up a system of laws and blood sacrifices to help his people recognize and deal with sin. Everything was arranged according to a pattern, and that pattern was a picture of the perfect sacrifice of Jesus Christ (Hebrews 9:6–14). The image of the Lamb of God as a sacrifice for sin appears also in Isaiah, where we are described as straying sheep. Our sin was laid on Jesus who *'was led like a lamb to the slaughter, and as a sheep before her shearers is silent, so he did not open his mouth'* (Isaiah 53:7).

In the shed blood of Jesus:

1. We have forgiveness for sin. *'In him we have redemption through his blood, the forgiveness of sins'* (Ephesians 1:7). (See also Matthew 26:28, Romans 3:25, Colossians 1:14 and Hebrews 9:23–28.)
2. We have cleansing and freedom (1 John 1:7 and Revelation 1:5).
3. God paid a supremely high price to purchase us for himself (1 Peter 1:18–19; Acts 20:28; Revelation 5:9).
4. We have been justified in God's sight and saved from his wrath (Romans 5:9).
5. God has brought us near to him, made peace with us, and reconciled all things to himself (Ephesians 2:13–16; Colossians 1:20–21).

6.   He has opened the way for us to come boldly in to God's presence (Hebrews 10:19-23).

7.   We have communion with God and eternal life (John 6:53-56).

8.   We have victory over Satan (Revelation 12:11).

In Exodus 12 the blood of the Lamb delivered the Israelites from judgment and death. God told them to sacrifice an unblemished lamb and to put its blood on the doorframes of their houses. They were to stay indoors and eat it hurriedly with their shoes on. When the Lord struck down all the first born of Egypt in judgment, he passed over the homes where he found blood of the lamb on the doorposts. The blood of the lamb delivered them from death. The blood of Jesus the Lamb not only delivers us from death, but also gives us eternal life. *'Whoever eats my flesh and drinks my blood has eternal life, and I will raise him up at the last day'* (John 6:54).

How we need to have a clear understanding of the tremendous power of Jesus' blood! We need to grasp just how much God given us through the blood sacrifice of Jesus. *'He who did not spare his own Son, but gave him up for us all – how will he not also, along with him, graciously give us all things?'* (Romans 8:32). May all that God has provided through the blood of Jesus Christ be ours in understanding and by experience.

Many Christians 'cover' things with the blood of Jesus in prayer, usually for protection against demonic attack. When I am uncertain of the source of thoughts or words of knowledge that come to me while praying, I place them under the blood of Jesus. Some of these thoughts quickly dissolve away, and I believe that these are not from the Lord. The ones from the Lord seem to strengthen rather than fade. In my experience of praying for deliverance, songs or scriptures which mention the blood of Jesus often stir up and help dislodge demons. The blood of Jesus and celebrating the Lord's supper are especially effective against the spirits of death and destruction.

2. The Word of Their Testimony

> *'But in your hearts set apart Christ as Lord. Always be prepared to give an answer to everyone who asks you to give the reason for the hope that you have.'*
>
> (1 Peter 3:15)

While reading an anthology of interviews with Chinese Christians, I repeatedly ran across sentences like 'She has a good testimony'. The writers meant that the person had been through much suffering and trouble, and yet had found victory in the Lord. 'There are some brothers and sisters in the prisons who die for God. They have beautiful testimonies for God because, during all their time in prison, all they had to do was deny God and they could have been freed. But they didn't do this.'[1] As I read through the book, I began to understand that such testimonies are costly, precious and powerful.

What does it take to become a witness? It is very simple. A witness is someone who has seen or heard something and can tell about it. Jesus told his followers that the power of the Holy Spirit would transform them into witnesses, *'But you will receive power when the Holy Spirit comes on you; and you will be my witnesses in Jerusalem, and in all Judea and Samaria, and to the ends of the earth'* (Acts 1:8). We will be **his** witnesses. Jesus Christ himself is always the focus of our testimony. God intends that we be filled with experiences of Jesus Christ. May we become like Peter and John, who were so full of the life of Jesus Christ, that when ordered by the Sanhedrin to stop speaking and teaching about him replied, *'. . . we cannot help speaking about what we have seen and heard'* (Acts 4:20).

People can argue philosophical and theological issues endlessly, but no one can argue with a testimony. We either believe the witness or not. What defense is there against the testimony of witnesses? Criminal gangs sometimes try to intimidate or assassinate witnesses. Lawyers investigate every aspect of the witness's life, painstakingly searching for anything that might call the witness's integrity into question. When the witness testifies, the lawyers search for inconsistencies in an attempt to discredit or weaken the testimony. Lawyers may ask questions designed to confuse the witness or make him falter or contradict himself. But a truthful, consistent testimony given by credible witnesses is powerful enough to acquit the innocent and condemn the guilty.

Satan tries to silence the faithful witnesses of Jesus Christ. He might attempt to **defuse** the testimony through fear, discouragement or shame. He might try to **discredit** the witness by drawing him into sin or through slander and false accusation. He might even try to **destroy** the witness. This strategy often backfires, however, because the testimony of martyred witnesses is very powerful. Clear, uncompromising testimony of Jesus Christ backed up with the witness's life leaves Satan defeated.

We believers seem to be subject to two particular problems when we give testimony for Jesus Christ – shame and fear. The Lord has addressed them both.

The well-educated Paul, a Roman citizen and former Jewish official, understood this problem well. He recognized that *'the message of the cross is foolishness to those who are perishing'* (1 Corinthians 1:18). He knew that the power of his testimony lay not in his wisdom and oratory style, but in the message of the cross of Christ Jesus itself. Paul declared, *'I am not ashamed of the gospel, because it is the power of God for the salvation of everyone who believes...'* (Romans 1:16). Paul, the prisoner, wrote advising Timothy, '*So do not be ashamed to testify about our Lord, or ashamed of me his prisoner. But join with me in suffering for the gospel, by the power of God*' (2 Timothy 1:8). In spite of his imprisonment, Paul declared, '*Yet I am not ashamed, because I know who I have believed, and am convinced that he is able to guard what I have entrusted to him for that day*' (2 Timothy 1:12).

Everyone who has tried to give testimony for Jesus has probably experienced the dry mouth, butterfly stomach (or even nausea), weak knees, and shaking hands that we associate with fear. Jesus expected that his witnesses would be called to testify in less than friendly circumstances.

> '*On my account you will be brought before governors and kings as witnesses to them and to the Gentiles.*'
> (Matthew 10:18)

> '*Whenever you are arrested and brought to trial, do not worry beforehand about what to say. Just say whatever is given you at the time, for it is not you speaking, but the Holy Spirit.*'
> (Mark 13:11)

What a frightening prospect for ordinary believers – being arrested and dragged into court or before rulers to give testimony. Jesus did not say 'if' you are arrested, but 'whenever'. But what a marvelous promise he gives – the Holy Spirit will give us what to say because God himself will speak through us. We will not be left to stutter along on our own. What comfort to banish our fear.

3. They Loved not Their Lives so Much as to Shrink from Death

> '. . . *I will go to the king, even though it is against the law. And if I perish, I perish.*'
> (Esther 4:16)

Queen Esther was probably tempted to keep quiet. She

had won a beauty contest and was selected as queen. Everything went smoothly until Haman, who hated the Jews, arranged an edict stating that all the Jews living in Media and Persia were to be robbed and murdered on a certain day. No one at the palace knew that Esther was Jewish. She could just keep a low profile until things settled down. To approach her husband, King Xerxes, was dangerous. The penalty for calling on him without being summoned was death. It was not only dangerous, but was probably also useless. Everyone knew that no edict could be rescinded or amended.

Esther entered the king's presence at the risk of her life and confessed her identity in order to intercede on behalf of her fellow Jews. She turned her back on fear and laid aside the shame being associated with a despised minority. The Jews were granted permission to fight for their lives and property, and they were saved. To this day Esther is remembered with a book of the Bible and a Jewish festival.

> Father, make me one who overcomes Satan and brings glory to Jesus. Teach me to understand and appropriate the blood of Jesus Christ. Through the power of your Holy Spirit, give me a good testimony. Grant me boldness to witness in the face of opposition. Make me as unashamed of the gospel as Paul. Make me as willing as Esther to lay down my own life in love and obedience.

Notes

1. *Wise as Serpents, Harmless as Doves – Chinese Christians Tell Their Stories*, by Jonathan Chao and Richard Van Houten. William Carey Library and China Graduate School of Theology, Pasadena and Hong Kong, 1988, p. 6.

Chapter 7

Avoiding the Enemy's Weapons

'The LORD said to Satan, "The LORD rebuke you, Satan! The LORD, who has chosen Jerusalem, rebuke you!"'
(Zechariah 3:2)

Satan, the Devil – what picture comes to mind? A comical figure in red pajamas with horns and a pitchfork? A 'ghost' with white hair and blue eyes? When we think of him are we amused or gripped with fear? What is he really like and how should we respond? There are excellent books which deal extensively with Satan's origins, personality, activities, and fate.[1] Here, we will look briefly at how the Bible describes Satan's personality and behavior.

While we certainly do not want to become party to *'Satan's so-called deep secrets'* (Revelation 2:24), neither should we be *'unaware of his schemes'* (2 Corinthians 2:11). Armed with an understanding of Satan's character and weapons, we will be able to avoid trying to use them.

Satan stands in rebellion against God, and he seeks to usurp God's place. He wants to sit on God's throne and draw all attention and worship to himself. He tries to disrupt God's good plans and purposes for his creation. Satan hates humans because we bear the image of our Creator. He especially hates God's people and wants to destroy them. Around Christians he prefers to work undetected.

Deceiver

> *'You belong to your father, the devil, and you want to carry out your father's desire. He was a murderer from the beginning, not holding to the truth, for there is no truth in him. When he lies, he speaks his native language, for he is a liar and the father of lies.'*
>
> (John 8:44)

Satan is the source of all lies and deception. He sows doubt about God's goodness and distorts our perception of God's character. He lies to us about God, ourselves, and everyone else. Scripture declares that Satan *'leads the whole world astray'* (Revelation 12:9). He *'denies that Jesus is the Christ,'* and *'he denies the Father and the Son'* (1 John 2:22). Satan deceives not only through lies, but he also tries to gain a following through *'all kinds of counterfeit miracles, signs and wonders'* (2 Thessalonians 2:9). He keeps his identity cloaked and *'masquerades as an angel of light'* (2 Corinthians 11:14).

Our prayers and intercession must be in truth. We need to let God deal with the depths of our hearts. Sin is deceitful, and when we are hardened by unconfessed sin, we are more susceptible to deception (Hebrews 3:13). We need to let God fill us with light and expose our true motivation. We must deal ruthlessly with our own hypocrisy. How many times do we pray nice-sounding words which are far from the true thoughts of our hearts? How often have we prayed 'nice' prayers to gain the approval of others? Whom do we think we are kidding? Do we think God cannot see through our masquerade? If we are not scrupulously truthful as we pray before God and with one another, how can our prayers come before him who lives in unapproachable light and whose name is the Truth?

Any time our prayers are tainted with lies or deception, we have been tricked. We are not holding God's weapon, but Satan's. Rather than giving expression to the will of God through prayer, we have played into Satan's hand and have become his tool.

Accuser

> *"The great dragon was hurled down – that ancient serpent called the devil, or Satan, who leads the whole world astray. He was hurled to the earth, and his angels with him.*
>
> *Then I heard a loud voice in heaven say: "Now have come the salvation and the power and the kingdom of our God, and the authority of his Christ. For the accuser of our brothers, who accuses them before our God day and night, has been hurled down."'*

(Revelation 12:10–11)

We first find Satan standing before the Lord bringing accusation in Job 1:6–12 and 2:1–6. There is a similar scene in Zechariah 3:1–5. Joshua, the high priest, is standing before the angel of the Lord, and Satan stands at his right side to accuse him.

It appears that Satan has now been barred from heaven and is confined to the earth (Revelation 12:7–12). If Satan has been expelled from heaven, how can he continue accusing believers before God? The truth is, we often do it for him. While Satan may be barred from heaven, we are invited *'to enter the Most Holy Place by the blood of Jesus . . . and to draw near to God'* (Hebrews 10:19, 22). When we come before the Lord, how will we pray? Will we be intercessors or accusers? [2]

What about prayers like, 'Dear Lord, please help Mary not to be so angry'? Are not such prayers merely thinly cloaked accusations? If we are to avoid representing Satan before the throne of God, we must make sure our prayer is free from accusation. We must be led by the Holy Spirit, rather than by our own perceptions, opinions or judgments.

When I shared this in a group of potential intercessors, one objected, 'If I do what you say, I won't have anything to pray.'

'That's OK,' I answered. 'Wait. Listen to God. Invite the Holy Spirit to show you what to pray.' When we lay aside our problem-oriented approach to prayer, we may have nothing to pray. May we admit we do not know how to pray, and may we allow the Holy Spirit to lead us into prayer that is free from accusation.

Other forms of accusation we must avoid are gossip and slander. Gossip is 'idle talk ... especially about the private affairs of others.'[3] I cannot find anywhere in scripture where it says gossip is allowable so long as we pray after we gossip. Praying for the personal needs of others should be done in the privacy of our prayer closets. Sharing information about someone's personal affairs should be done only with permission and ideally by request. Much damage has been done in the body of Christ through 'intercessors' who have failed to respect the privacy of others. The same person who would never share such things over coffee will do so all too freely when it is 'for prayer'. Gossiping 'for prayer' is still gossip, and it plays into the hands of the enemy. What makes us think we can pray effectively when our prayers are based on broken confidence and a form of accusation?

'To slander' means 'to defame' or 'to malign'.[4] Slander does not **have** to be false to be slander. Whether true or false, it sullies someone's reputation. When we slander someone, we spread a bad report about them. Psalm 15 makes the Lord's opinion of slander very clear.

> *'LORD, who may dwell in your sanctuary?*
> *Who may live on your holy hill?*
> *He whose walk is blameless*
> *and who does what is righteous,*
> *who speaks the truth from his heart*
> *and has no slander on his tongue,*
> *who does his neighbor no wrong*
> *and casts no slur on his fellow man'*
>
> (Psalm 15:1–3)[5]

May we come to the Lord for healing and deliverance from everything that attracts us to malicious talk – our wounds and insecurity, our envy and ambition, our pride and guilt, and our curiosity and love of gossip and scandal. May we agree before God and one another that we will not gossip and slander in the name of prayer. May we covenant with one another to neither speak nor listen to such talk. May we gently and lovingly hold one another accountable in the Lord.

Murderer

> *'. . . he was a murderer from the beginning . . .'*
>
> (John 8:44)

Jesus said Satan is a murderer. He is full of malice and *'is filled with fury'* (Revelation 12:12). His weapons include anger, rage and violence. There is no love in him, but he is filled with hatred.

Especially when directly confronting Satan or his minions, it is easy to be drawn into prayer that is tainted with anger, hatred and violence. God wants us to *'lift up holy hands in prayer, without anger or disputing'*

(1 Timothy 2:8). Our motive for prayer must be nothing less than a heart filled with the compassion of Christ, a heart desiring that the Father's will be done. When our motivation is pure, so will our prayer be.

Some Christians, when coming against satanic strong-holds, engage in angry name-calling and violent prayer, pronouncing graphic imprecations against Satan. Make no mistake – Satan has been around for a long time. He is the undisputed master of evil. He is the *summa cum laude* of malice, hatred and violence. These are his weapons, and he knows them thoroughly. Satan is also an expert on fallen human nature. He has probed our weaknesses for thousands of years. There is no way we can take up Satan's weapons and successfully wield them against him. They are his weapons and he is the expert.

In contrast, the weapons God gives us are based upon his own character. Satan cannot understand them. He has no defense against things like love, faithfulness, submission and gentleness.

Facing the Enemy

> *'But even the archangel Michael, when he was disputing with the devil about the body of Moses, did not dare to bring a slanderous accusation against him, but said, "The Lord rebuke you!"'*   (Jude 9)

In dealing with Satan, we must avoid Satan's weapons. We must especially avoid bringing a slanderous accusation against him. I have occasionally heard people praying, calling Satan a dirty so-and-so and accusing him of all kinds of evil. People who pray or speak this way are in very bad company. Consider these passages:

> *'This is especially true of those who follow the corrupt desire of the sinful nature and despise authority.*

Bold and arrogant, these men are not afraid to slander celestial beings; yet even angels, although they are stronger and more powerful, do not bring slanderous accusations against such beings in the presence of the Lord. But these men blaspheme in matters they do not understand.

They are like brute beasts, creatures of instinct, born only to be caught and destroyed, and like beasts they too will perish. They will be paid back with harm for the harm they have done. Their idea of pleasure is to carouse in broad daylight. They are blots and blemishes, reveling in their pleasures while they feast with you. With eyes full of adultery, they never stop sinning; they seduce the unstable; they are experts in greed – an accursed brood! They have left the straight way and wandered off to follow the way of Balaam son of Beor, who loved the wages of wickedness. But he was rebuked for his wrongdoing by a donkey – a beast without speech – who spoke with a man's voice and restrained the prophet's madness.

These men are springs without water and mists driven by a storm. Blackest darkness is reserved for them. For they mouth empty, boastful words and, by appealing to the lustful desires of sinful human nature, they entice people who are just escaping from those who live in error. They promise them freedom, while they themselves are slaves of depravity – for a man is a slave to whatever has mastered him.'

(2 Peter 2:10–19)

'In the very same way, these dreamers pollute their own bodies, reject authority and slander celestial beings. But even the archangel Michael, when he was disputing with the devil about the body of Moses, did not dare to bring a slanderous accusation against him, but *said, "The Lord rebuke you!" Yet these men speak abusively against whatever they do not understand; and what things they do understand by instinct, like unreasoning animals – these are the very things that destroy them.*

Woe to them! They have taken the way of Cain; they have rushed for profit into Balaam's error; they have been destroyed in Korah's rebellion.

These men are blemishes at your love feasts, eating with you without the slightest qualm – shepherds who feed only themselves. They are clouds without rain, blown along by the wind; autumn trees, without fruit and uprooted – twice dead. They are wild waves of the sea, foaming up their shame; wandering stars, for whom blackest darkness has been reserved forever.'

(Jude 8–13)

Enough said? Let us not join with those who slander celestial beings. But how do we come against Satan? Should we say only, 'The Lord rebuke you?' Certainly we are not more powerful than the archangel Michael. We humans are undoubtedly weaker than even the weakest angel. We are no match for Satan, but we do not stand against him on our own. We have been authorized and sent by Jesus Christ himself.

'The seventy-two returned with joy and said, "Lord, even the demons submit to us in your name."

He replied, "I saw Satan fall like lightning from heaven. I have given you authority to trample on snakes and scorpions and to overcome all the power of the enemy; nothing will harm you. However, do not rejoice that the spirits submit to you, but rejoice that your names are written in heaven."'

(Luke 10: 17–20)

This passage makes me think of a small boy I saw in a movie. Harassed by a group of older boys every day on his way to and from school, he lived in terror and humiliation. One day, the little boy gathered his courage and stood up to them. To his complete surprise, the bullies ran away. The delighted boy did not realize that his enormous family dog had been standing right behind him. We are a bit like that little boy. Hopelessly weak on our own, we are backed up by the One who is sovereign over all. In Christ Jesus we always triumph, and Satan knows it. Yet we are instructed to rejoice instead that our names are written in heaven.

> *'I will sing of your love and justice; to you, O LORD, I will sing praise. I will be careful to lead a blameless life – when will you come to me? I will walk in my house with blameless heart. I will set before my eyes no vile thing ... I will have nothing to do with evil. Whoever slanders his neighbor in secret, him will I put to silence'* (Psalm 101:1–3, 5).

Father in heaven, when I come before your throne of grace, may it always be to seek your grace. Protect me from deception and free me from lies. May I never seek to intercede with anger or violence, and may I never bring a slanderous accusation. Preserve me in the shadow of your wing. Deliver me from pride and arrogance. When I face the enemy, may I always remember who is standing behind me.

Notes

1. For example, *The Adversary*, by Mark Bubeck. Moody Press, Chicago, 1975 or *The Screwtape Letters*, by C.S. Lewis. Collins, Glasgow, 1982.

2. This idea comes from an excellent article, 'The Two Ministries',
    by Rick Joyner, *The Morning Star*. MorningStar Publications,
    PO Box 369, Pineville, NC 28134, Vol. 1, No. 1, p. 5–13.
3. *Random House Webster's Electronic Dictionary and Thesaurus*,
    Version 1.20, cv 'gossip'. Reference Software International, San
    Francisco, 1991.
4. *Ibid.*, cv 'slander'.
5. For other references to 'gossip' and 'slander', see also Matthew
    15:19, Ephesians 4:31, and James 4:11.

Chapter 8

Gideon and the Weapons of God

'God is With You, Mighty Warrior'

Before you read this chapter, it will be helpful to read Judges 6–8. In Gideon's day, the nation of Israel was in serious trouble. The Israelites did what was evil in God's sight, so he allowed their enemies to invade the land and oppress them. It was a terrible time. They ran into the mountains and hid anywhere they could – in shelters, in caves and even in cracks in the rocks. Whenever they planted crops, nomadic tribes from the East swarmed over the land with huge herds of livestock and destroyed everything. This went on for seven years. Frightened and impoverished, the Israelites cried out to God for help.

God heard the cries of his people and sent a prophet who identified the cause of Israel's problem. '"I am the LORD your God; do not worship the gods of the Amorites, in whose land you live." But you have not listened to me' (Judges 6:10). Besides graciously giving the Israelites an opportunity to repent of their idolatry, God also took action. He visited Gideon, 'When the angel of the Lord appeared to Gideon, he said, "The LORD is with you, mighty warrior"' (Judges 6:12). Where was this mighty warrior and what was he doing? Gideon was busy threshing wheat. But instead of threshing on a threshing floor, a windy hilltop, Gideon was trying to do the job while hiding in the bottom of a winepress because he was afraid of the Midianites.[1]

> '"Go in the strength you have and save Israel out of Midian's hand," God commanded, "Am I not sending you?"'
> (Judges 6:14)

Strength? What strength? Gideon pointed out that he was not exactly the mighty warrior type: '... "how can I save Israel? My clan is the weakest in Manasseh, and I am the least in my family"' (Judges 6:15). God answered simply, '"I will be with you... "' (Judges 6:16).

When God called Gideon, he called him *'mighty warrior'*. With God's call came God's strength and means – the presence of God himself. We are a lot like Gideon – ordinary people just trying to get through the day – no one important or powerful. And we are the kind of people God still calls.

> *Brothers, think of what you were when you were called. Not many of you were wise by human standards; not many were influential; not many were of noble birth. But God chose the foolish things of the world to shame the wise; God chose the weak things of the world to shame the strong. He chose the lowly things of this world and the despised things – and the things that are not – to nullify the things that are, so that no one may boast before him.'*
> (1 Corinthians 1:26–29)

Are you just an ordinary person, no one special? God is calling you, mighty warrior. And with his call is his promise: *'Never will I leave you; never will I forsake you'* (Hebrews 13:5). Alone we are weak, helpless and can do nothing. But we are not alone – God himself, Emmanuel, is with us. This is how ordinary, fearful, weak people are transformed into God's mighty warriors.

The Lord directed Gideon to tear down his father's idolatrous altar and build a proper one to the Lord God. Because he was afraid of his family and the townspeople, he did it at night. He was afraid, but he obeyed. The next morning the people wanted to put him to death. But Gideon's father pointed out that a god ought to be able to defend himself, so they decided to leave the matter to their pagan god, Baal.

God is calling us, like Gideon, to tear down our idolatrous altars. Perhaps we come from a family that worships idols. We must make a complete break with our old ways. We must not compromise in order to appease our family and neighbors.

Mei-yan is the pastor of a small church in Hong Kong. A seminary graduate, she knows how to preach and minister in a church setting. But for many years she has struggled with prayer and hearing God's voice. No amount of effort on her part or prayer by others seemed to help. Her problem eventually caused her to become dependent upon a prayer partner who would 'hear' God's voice for her.

For many years Mei-yan lived with her mother who was an avid idol worshipper. Her mother celebrated all the popular local festivals and burned incense to all kinds of spirits. Even after Mei-yan became a Christian, she was often present during these home worship ceremonies.

'Did you participate? Did you eat the offerings?' I asked her.

'Well, yes,' she answered. 'Paul said that an idol is nothing, so it is all right to eat the sacrifices so long as it doesn't disturb your conscience or make someone else stumble.' Without hesitation she turned to 1 Corinthians 8:4–13 and read it to support her position.

'Yes,' I answered, 'but Paul also says that the person who eats the sacrifices participates at the altar.' I turned to 1 Corinthians 10: 18–21 and read, *'Do not those who eat the sacrifices participate in the altar? Do I mean then that a sacrifice offered to an idol is anything, or that an idol is anything? No, but the sacrifices of pagans are offered to demons, not to God, and I do not want you to be participants with demons. You cannot drink the cup of the Lord and the cup of demons too; you cannot have part in both the Lord's table and the table of demons.'*

This passage, only a page away, had somehow escaped Mei-yan's notice. How true that both the idol and the one bound to it have *'their eyes . . . plastered over so they cannot see, and their minds closed so they cannot understand'* (Isaiah 44:18). With the help of a Bible commentary, we looked at how the two passages could be harmonized. Convinced that she had participated in idol worship, Mei-yan repented and asked God for forgiveness. Then we prayed that her eyes, ears and understanding would be opened so she could hear God's voice.

While most Westerners do not worship actual idols, they may still be bound by idolatry. An idol is anything that we place before our devotion and obedience to the Lord. *'For where your treasure is, there your heart will be also'* (Matthew 6:21). What is our first priority? Money? Possessions? Success? Recognition? Prestige? A comfortable life? Education? A secure future for our family? While these things are not wrong in themselves, what have we put in first place? Are there some idolatrous altars that we need to tear down? Maybe they came from our family or our society, but it is time to tear them down and build a proper one to the Lord.

217

Only Willing Warriors

> *'The* LORD *says to my Lord:*
> *"Sit at my right hand*
> *until I make your enemies*
> *a footstool for your feet."*
> *The* LORD *will extend your mighty scepter from Zion;*
> *you will rule in the midst of your enemies.*
> *Your troops will be willing*
> *on your day of battle.'*   (Psalm 110:1–3)

Things quieted down for Gideon until all the tribes from the east joined forces and crossed the Jordan into Israel again. *'Then the Spirit of the* LORD *came upon Gideon, and he blew a trumpet'* and sent messages, calling a number of tribes to arms. The blast of his trumpet assembled an army of 32,000 fighting men (Judges 6:34–35).

Not bad, but how big was the invading army? A look at Judges 8:10 and a quick calculation tells us that the eastern peoples had an army of 135,000 men. Does 32,000 seem like enough now? But God told Gideon he had too many! God wanted to make sure Israel would not be able to boast that her own strength had saved her (Judges 7:2).

God told Gideon to announce, *'Anyone who trembles with fear may turn back and leave Mount Gilead. So twenty-two thousand men left, while ten thousand remained'* (Judges 7:3). Those who were incapacitated by fear were simply excused.

Anyone mustering an earthly army will tell you this strategy is absurd. Troops have to be drafted, sometimes at gun-point. God, however, intended Israel to be different. God's strategy for raising an army is found in Deuteronomy 20:1–9. First, the people were told not to be afraid when facing powerful enemies. The priests were to tell them,

> '*"Hear, O Israel, today you are going into battle against your enemies. Do not be fainthearted or afraid; do not be terrified or give way to panic before them. For the Lord your God is the one who goes with you to fight for you against your enemies to give you victory."*'   (Deuteronomy 20:3–4)

Next the officers were to address the people, excusing those who had just built houses but had not dedicated them, those who had planted vineyards but had not yet enjoyed them, and those who were pledged to be married. The officers were then to add, '*"Is any man afraid or fainthearted? Let him go home so that his brothers will not become disheartened too"*' (Deuteronomy 20:8).

Anyone unwilling to fight could be excused for any number of reasons. Although all were commanded not to be afraid, anyone who was afraid was not compelled to go into battle. Everyone was free to go home, no questions asked. God's army was to be made up only of willing warriors.

What an unusual army and how unlike the armies of this world. But God had called Israel to be special. '*For you are a people holy to the LORD your God. The LORD your God has chosen you out of all the peoples on the face of the earth to be his people, his treasured possession*' (Deuteronomy 7:6).

Then God's word came to Gideon again – there were still too many men. God gave further instructions and when the selection had been completed, Gideon had an army of only three hundred men. Three hundred facing 135,000. Any victory would unquestionably belong to the Lord and no one would be able to boast.

Today, God is assembling a Gideon's army of intercessors, an army of willing warriors. Those who hear the trumpet are responding. They are ordinary believers, no one special or important. They are assembling for battle.

Their numbers are small compared to the enemy gathered against them. But they are determined not to give way to fear. No one will be able to claim victory in his own strength. As the battle is the Lord's, so is the victory. Do you hear the trumpet? *'God is with you, mighty warrior.'*

Torches and Broken Jars

Following God's instructions, Gideon assembled his men in the middle of the night, divided them into three companies, and gave them their weapons. Each soldier received an empty jar, a burning torch and a trumpet. The jars and torches were in their left hands and the trumpets in their right. Gideon instructed them to watch, follow his lead and shout, *'For the LORD and for Gideon'* (Judges 7:18). Gideon's men took up positions around the enemy camp. At Gideon's signal they blew their trumpets,[2] broke their jars, raised their torches, shouted,[3] and held their positions. God did the rest, and an army of 135,000 was routed by three hundred men who had not even drawn their swords.

Gideon and his men fought a spiritual battle with spiritual weapons, and these are relevant for us today. Gideon's men carried jars – earthen pots commonly used for carrying or storing water. These were common pots put to an uncommon use. Scripture often refers to people also as earthen vessels or clay in the hands of God, the master potter.[4] God shapes us; we are his workmanship. Through ordinary people, God does extraordinary things.

Gideon's men each carried a burning torch, a light. Jesus, *'the light of the world'* (John 8:12), is the treasure inside the clay jars, inside us. *'For God ... made his light shine in our hearts to give us the light of the knowledge of the glory of God in the face of Christ. But we have this treasure in jars of clay to show that this all-surpassing power is from God and not from us'* (2 Corinthians 4:6–7). The jars are weak in themselves, but they contain a treasure – Jesus lives inside.

But look what happened! The soldiers broke their clay jars. This was the point of no return. Before the men broke their jars, their presence was a secret, and they were concealed in the darkness. They could have crept away undetected. However, once their jars were broken, their presence and positions became obvious to the enemy. There could be no going back.

Each man's decision to break his jar and raise his torch was an individual one. Let us stand for a moment with Gideon's men on the edge of the Midianite camp.

The enormous enemy camp is spread out in the valley below. There are no sentries – who would be crazy enough to attack such a huge army? A mere three hundred of us rim the hills in the darkness, but I am alone – I cannot see the others. I believe God has sent us here, that this is his battle. Conscious of the trumpet in my right hand I remember the Lord's promise, *'When you go into battle in your own land against an enemy who is oppressing you, sound a blast on the trumpets. Then you will be remembered by the LORD your God and rescued from your enemies'* (Numbers 10:9). I believe the Lord's promise, but as I look out over the hordes, I know there is no earthly way I can come out of this alive. I have already made my decision, though. I choose to walk by faith rather than by sight. As torch lights blaze forth in the darkness along the rims of the surrounding hills, I hear trumpet blasts and shouts. Without hesitation I break my jar, raise my torch, and press the trumpet to my lips.

'For God, who said, "Let light shine out of darkness," made his light shine in our hearts to give us the light of the knowledge of the glory of God in the face of Christ.

But we have this treasure in jars of clay to show that this all-surpassing power is from God and not from us. We are hard pressed on every side, but not crushed; perplexed, but not in despair; persecuted, but not abandoned; struck down, but not destroyed. We always carry around in our body the death of Jesus, so that the life of Jesus may also be revealed in our body. For we who are alive are always being given over to death for Jesus' sake, so that his life may be revealed in our mortal body. So then, death is at work in us, but life is at work in you.'   (2 Corinthians 4:7–12)

Only broken jars display the light. Jesus invites us to come, be filled with his light and break our jars. He asks us to lay down our lives so his light can shine out through us. It is an invitation to come and die. This is the message of the gospel, *'Then Jesus said to his disciples, "If anyone would come after me, he must deny himself and take up his cross and follow me. For whoever wants to save his life will lose it, but whoever loses his life for me will find it"'* (Matthew 16:24–25). God has called us to give up our own lives and live his (Galatians 2:20).

Gideon and his men broke their jars, held up their torches, blew trumpets and shouted. As each man blew his trumpet, they individually and corporately called upon the Lord. Obedient to the Lord's instructions, each man shouted. They did not just stand there waiting to be noticed by the enemy. They went on the offensive.

God is calling forth an army of willing warriors, a Gideon's army of intercessors, people who have counted the cost and decided not to give way to fear. They are like the people mentioned in Revelation 12:11 who *'overcame [Satan] by the blood of the Lamb and by the word of their testimony; they did not love their lives so much as to shrink from death.'* They are willing to step forward and stand in the gaps – in the broken-down places, the wounded spots – of the body of Christ, of our society, cities, nations and world. These are the weak ones, but God's Spirit is upon them. Do you hear this call? *'God is with you, mighty warrior.'*

Father in heaven, I hear the spiritual trumpet call to arms. Under the direction of your Holy Spirit, I commit myself to intercession and spiritual warfare. By your grace and power, enable me to stand firm in the face of the enemy. Lord, I choose to take up my cross and follow you. Help me to break my jar, boldly hold forth your light, call upon you, and take a stand against the enemy. Lord, teach me to pray. May I *'always carry around in [my] body the death of Jesus, so that the life of Jesus may also be revealed in [my] body'* (2 Corinthians 4:10). Father, may Jesus be glorified through me, so that he may be lifted up and all men may be drawn unto him. Amen.

Notes

1. *Zondervan Pictorial Bible Dictionary*, Merrill C. Tenney, Ed., Zondervan Publishing House, Grand Rapids, MI, 1973, pp. 850, 895.
2. Trumpets are used in the Bible: to call to war, Judges 6:34 (Gideon); in war, Joshua 6:1–5, 20 (Jericho); for warning, Ezekiel 33:1–7 (watchmen); in worship, 2 Chronicles 29:25–28, Joel 2:15–17; in celebration, 2 Chronicles 20:27–29; in proclamation of a king, 1 Kings 1:32–35. (1 Corinthians 14:6–12 uses trumpet imagery to encourage Christians to exercise spiritual gifts to edify the church.)
3. Shouting is used in battle: Joshua 6:1–5,20; in worship and praise and the ascension of the king, Psalm 47, esp. verses 1 and 5.
4. For example: Job 10:9, 33:6, Isaiah 29:16, 45:9, Jeremiah 18:5–6, 19:1 and Romans 9:21.

For Further Reading

Bubeck, Mark I., *The Adversary*. Moody Press, Chicago. 1975.

Dawson, John, *Taking our Cities for God*. Creation House, Lake Mary, FL. 1989.

Frangipane, Francis, *The House of the Lord*. Creation House, Lake Mary, FL. 1991.

Frangipane, Francis, *The Three Battlegrounds*. Advancing Church Publications, River of Life Ministries, PO Box 10102, Cedar Rapids, Iowa, 52410. 1989.

Huggett, Joyce, *Listening to God*. Hodder and Stoughton, London. 1986.

Joyner, Rick, *There Were Two Trees in the Garden*. Whitaker House, Springdale, PA. 1993.

Matthews, Aurthur, *Born for Battle*. Send the Light and Overseas Missionary Fellowship, Carlisle. 1978.

Murray, Andrew, *The Ministry of Intercession*. Whitaker House, Springdale, PA. 1982.

Prince, Derek, *Shaping History Through Prayer and Fasting*. Whitaker House, Springdale, PA. 1973.

Ravenhill, Leonard, *Revival God's Way*. Bethany House, Minneapolis. 1983.

Wagner, Elizabeth, *Tearing Down Strongholds – Prayer for Buddhists*. Living Books for All, Christian Literature Crusade, Hong Kong. 1988.

Wallis, Arthur, *Pray in the Spirit*. Kingsway, Eastbourne. 1970.

Wallis, Arthur, *God's Chosen Fast*. Kingsway, Eastbourne. 1968.

White, Tom, *The Believer's Guide to Spiritual Warfare*. Kingsway, Eastbourne. 1991.

If you have enjoyed this book and would like to help us to send a copy of it and many other titles to needy pastors in the **Third World,** please write for further information or send your gift to:

**Sovereign World Trust
PO Box 777, Tonbridge
Kent TN11 9XT
United Kingdom**

or to the **'Sovereign World'** distributor in your country.

If sending money from outside the United Kingdom, please send an International Money Order or Foreign Bank Draft in STERLING, drawn on a **UK** bank to **Sovereign World Trust.**